Homage to
William Shakespeare
Richard Wagner

by Momen

Introductions by Erland Josephson
and James A. Mason

Agreka™ Books, Salt Lake City, Utah, USA

Karl Momen 1998
Published by Homage to the Classics Foundation

ISBN: 1-888-10684-0
Library of Congress 00-101112

Agreka™ Books, Salt Lake City, Utah, USA:
Tel. (800) 360-5284, Fax (888) 771-7758
www.utahbooks.com
Scandinavian distributor: Silander & Fromholtz Förlags AB, Sweden.
Tel. 08 662 90 50 Fax 08 662 90 51
sf@stockholm.mail.telia.com

Graphic design by Christian Wirsén, c.wirsen@swipnet.se
Photography by J. Daniel
Translation Björn Anzén

Front cover: *Henry V* by Momen
Back cover: *Das Rheingold* by Momen

Printed in Sweden by Wallin & Dalholm Boktryckeri AB, Lund. 2000.

I have read and listened to Shakespeare being performed in the German, Swedish, and English languages, hundreds of times. To comprehend philosophy one is best served with the knife-sharp and precise German language. But the majesty and grandeur of the English language, with the richness of its expression, renders Shakespeare's genius more versatile and his plays become prismatic. Each time one experiences a performance it is perceived through a different color of the many-faceted prism. The English language is my fourth language and with this handicap I cannot expect even a bronze medal, especially when I am fourth in line.

I express my appreciation and gratitude to those who who helped with the realization of this book *Erland Josephson* and *James A. Mason* for the Introductions, *Carl-Gustav Yrwing* for coordinating the project, *Herman Du Toit* for advice and editing, and *Dietrich Fischer Diskau* and *Robert W. Gutman* for use of some citations from their books *Wagner und Nietzsche* and *Wagner, the Man, His Mind and Music.*

Karl Momen

Mya

I hope this proves interesting and useful in your studies of Shakesphere.

Remember! x

Shakesphere is meant to be watched, not read

Enjoy! x

Love
Georgina

List of works in order of appearance.

Henry V, 1996	p. 14	170 x 170 cm
Richard III, 1996	p. 16	170 x 170 cm
Macbeth, 1996-97	p. 18	170 x 170 cm
Julius Cæsar, 1997	p. 20	170 x 170 cm
Anthony and Cleopatra, 1997	p. 22	170 x 170 cm
Othello, 1996	p. 24	170 x 170 cm
Romeo and Juliet, 1997-98	p. 26	170 x 170 cm
Hamlet, 1997	p. 28	170 x 170 cm
Das Rheingold, 1989-96	p. 36	150 x 200 cm
Die Walküre, 1996-98	p. 38	150 x 200 cm
Siegfried, 1989-90	p. 40	150 x 200 cm
Götterdämmerung, 1990-97	p. 42	150 x 200 cm
Lohengrin, 1997	p. 44	170 x 170 cm
Tristan und Isolde, 1997	p. 46	170 x 170 cm
Der Fliegende Holländer, 1998	p. 48	170 x 170 cm
Die Meistersinger von Nürenberg, 1998	p. 50	170 x 170 cm
Tannhäuser, 1997-98	p. 52	170 x 170 cm
Parsifal, 1998	p. 54	170 x 170 cm

MOMEN

Now and then people ask me why it is that I am so devoted to the theater, the opera, and to music. They question, "Surely, you were not born into the European culture?" When I reflect on this I feel like Sinbad the Sailor. I have crossed so many cultural borders, although born and raised in Mashhad in northern Iran, not far from the Caspian Sea and the Russian border. My cultural roots are a blend of ancient Persian traditions and Russian folklore. As a child I listened to my father reciting poetry and tales from pre-Islamic Persian mythology about heroes, kings, and demons. These tales were sometimes spiced with stories from Russian folklore.

Later I was surprised to learn how much ancient Persian mythology, with its tales of kings and heroes, was related to Nordic mythology. True, it could be said that the various heroes were shaped from the same matter, yet they were different. In the Nordic tales the gods were the center of focus, while the ancient Persian tales held the kings at center. The explanation for this is found in the fact that at the time of the creation of these tales, from about 650 B.C., the religion of Zarathustra applied. These fundamental differences in the folklore tradition are particularly evident in Wagner's "The Ring," which was based on Nordic mythology.

During my adolescence I read hundreds of novels by French, Russian, German, English, and American 18th and 19th century writers. However, in these early years I was not at all familiar with music, opera, or theater. These acquaintances were initiated when I came to Germany in order to study arts and architecture. Soon I became absorbed in the world of the opera and the theater as if into a black hole with a gravitational pull from which it was impossible to escape. In other words, it was a case of Paradise with Dante's Inferno in each corner.

Since 1961 I have resided in Sweden. My travels during the 1960s and 1970s, to various countries in Europe and the USA, gave me the opportunity to watch and listen to hundreds of plays in several different languages. The advantage of this was that I was able to experience a number of different nuances of interpretation of these plays. As a result I have acquired a rich and broad basis for my own interpretations.

By chance I discovered a small record company which had been recording the best plays in London's West End theaters as well as on Broadway during the years 1954-1964. Consequently, I acquired more than 150 recordings from Euripides' "Medea" to Sartre's "No Exit," and Becket's "Waiting for Godot." Sometimes I sense how privileged I am. What joy to be able to listen to these kings, angels, devils, oppressors, victims, the good, the bad, the comical, and the tragic. I can feel them near me, and when I hear them it is as if they are right in front of me. They are at my disposal and they share with me the wisdom of a thousand years; sane as well as insane thoughts, laughter, tears, hope, and despair. And I will not let them down. I cannot say that I fully understand all that they utter, often the content is complicated and these thousand year old thoughts may better be suited to a god or a philosopher, something which I am not. But I refuse to give in and I follow as best I can. I am already inside the door and no one can throw me out!

It was difficult to choose between all the operas and plays to find precisely that which I have been attempting to interpret in my paintings. I chose Shakespeare as his production is so extensive and valuable in its treatment of man's psychological and existential condition. I chose the operas of Wagner because I am fascinated by the mythological and musical diversity, and the richness of the world of fairy tales.

In Shakespeare I recognize all the imaginable situations and events that could be encountered.He reflects all human conditions from the darkest to the brightest, with rapid interchanges between the tragic and the comical. To represent any one of these human passions with my spectrum of colors is a difficult challenge. Shakespeare penetrates all man's evil and good characteristics. The Evil is released only when his characters are provoked or betrayed. The Evil is like a cloud of gas in anticipation of the spark that will ignite the explosion. Somehow Shakespeare allows us the knowledge that Evil will not act unless provoked by betrayal or by victimization of a character in the plot. In my painting I attempt to create a theatrical scenography with identical stages. Scenes are drawn out of the environment of the drama, with distinct features of character and symbolism, portraying the drama in abstract form. In the operas of Wagner I see a complete representation of "Gesamte Kunst." In contrast to many other operas one experiences image, theater, music, and word in a very distinct form. Yet from the beginning every character is represented by a musically identifiable sound, describing a person or an environment regardless of their existence or not. Nevertheless, you follow the action in a clear and obvious manner. The music of Wagner is very manifest in its description of joy, despair, love, cunning, and hate. Occasionally it is so manifest that words really are unnessary in order to grasp the psychological situations in the drama.

Restricted by the possibilities of painting I have attempted to represent my experiences of these spiritual giants of the theater and opera in distinct colors and symbolic abstract forms. I wish I could open the door to my inner being and visualize my dreams of them in a more extensive way than painting allows. Could it be possible in the future, through the wonders of technology, to materialize dreams?

Momen.

Swedish translation:

Från tid till annan frågar man mig hur det kommer sig att jag är så engagerad i teater, opera och musik och de säger, "Du är väl inte född med den europeiska kulturen"? Vid närmare eftertanke känner jag mig som Sindbad sjöfararen. Jag har vandrat över många kulturgränser, samtidigt som jag är född och uppvuxen i Meshed i norra Iran, inte långt från Kaspiska havet och den ryska gränsen. från Kaspiska havet och den ryska gränsen. Mina kulturella rötter är en blandning av urpersisk tradition och rysk folklore. Jag hörde som barn min far läsa dikter och sagor ur förislamisk persisk mytologi om hjältar, kungar och demoner. Ibland kryddade han dessa berättelser med historier ur ryska sagor.

Senare har jag förvånats över hur mycket den urpersiska mytologin, med sina sagor om kungar och hjältar, hör ihop med de nordiska myterna. Visserligen kan man säga att de olika hjältarna och kungarna är formade ur samma substans, men ändå skiljer de sig. I de nordiska sagorna var gudarna centralgestalter, medan kungarna stod i centrum i det antika Persiens sagor. Detta berodde på att, vid tiden för dessa sagors tillkomst, gällde Zarathustras religion, från 650-talet f.kr. Dessa fundamentala skillnader i sagotradition märks inte minst i Wagners "Ringen", som bygger på den nordiska mytologin.

Under mina tonår läste jag hundratals romaner av franska, ryska, tyska, engelska och amerikanska 1800- och 1900-talsförfattare. Vid denna tidpunkt hade jag emellertid inte fått minsta kontakt med musik, opera och teater.

Dessa möten skedde först när jag kom till Tyskland för att studera konst och arkitektur. Men snart nog blev jag indragen i denna värld av opera och teater som i ett svart hål med en gravitationskraft som gjorde det omöjligt att ta sig tillbaka. Med andra ord ett paradis med Dantes inferno i varje hörn.

Sedan 1961 är jag bosatt i Sverige. Under mina årliga resor under 60- och 70-talen till olika länder i Europa och USA, fick jag möjlighet att se och höra hundratals teaterföreställningar på olika språk. Fördelen med det var att jag upplevde många skilda tolkningar och nyanseringar av olika pjäser. Därigenom har jag fått en rik och bred bas för mina egna tolkningar.

Av ren slump fick jag kontakt med ett litet skivförlag, som från åren 1954–1964 hade spelat in de bästa teaterföreställningarna på West End i London och på Brodway i New York. Nu hade jag plötsligt mer än 150 inspelningar, alltifrån Euripides "MedeaC till Sartres "No Exit" och Beckets "I väntan på Godot".

Ibland känner jag hur priviligierad jag är, vilken lycka att kunna lyssna till dessa kungar, kejsare, änglar, djävlar, förtryckare, förtryckta, det goda, det onda, det komiska och det tragiska. Jag känner dem nära mig och när jag hör dem är det som om de stod framför mig. De står till mitt förfogande och de delar med sig av tusenårig visdom, kloka som vansinniga tankar, skratt, gråt, hopp och förtvivlan och jag sviker dem inte!!

Jag kan inte påstå att jag till fullo förstår allt vad som sägs, innehållet är många gånger komplicerat och dessa tusenåriga tankar är mer för en gud eller en filosof, något som jag absolut inte är. Dock ger jag inte upp utan hänger med så gott det går. Jag står redan innanför dörren och ingen kan visa ut mig.

Det är svårt att välja bland alla operor och teaterpjäser, att finna just det som jag försökt tolka i mina målningar. Shakespeare valde jag eftersom hans produktion är så omfattande och varierande och behandlar och analyserar människans psykologiska och existensiella situation. Wagners operor för att jag tycker om och fascineras av den mytologiska och musikaliska mångsidigheten och rikedomen i sagornas värld.

Hos Shakespeare känner jag igen alla tänkbara situationer och händelser som man kan råka ut för eller anar sig till. Han speglar alla mänskliga situationer från det mörkaste till det ljusaste, som kan växla häftigt mellan det tragiska och det komiska. Att söka någon av dessa mänskliga lidelser med mina färgspektra är både svårt och en utmaning.

Shakespeare genomskådar människans alla onda och goda sidor. Hos den onda karaktären släpps det onda loss först när han eller hon provoceras eller upplever sig sviken. Det onda är som ett gasmoln som väntar på en gnista för att explodera. På något sätt låter Shakespeare betraktaren veta att den ondskefulle inte agerar utan att ha blivit utsatt för besvikelse eller någon form av intrig.
På mina målningar försöker jag sätta upp teaterscener med exakt samma kulisser. Scener ur dramats miljöer med distinkta karaktärsdrag, i symbolisk form, får gestalta dramat i en abstrakt form.

I Wagners operor ser jag en fullständig framställning av "Gesamte Kunst". I motsats till många andra operor upplever man bild, teater, musik och ord i mycket distinkt form och från början separeras varenda karaktär i en musikaliskt identifierbar klang, som beskriver en person eller en miljö oavsett om de finns eller inte. Trots detta följer man handlingen på ett klart och tydligt sätt.

Wagners musik är mycket tydlig i sin beskrivning av glädje, förtvivlan, kärlek, list och hat. Ibland så tydlig att orden egentligen inte behövs för att uppfatta de psykologiska situationerna i dramat.
Jag har försökt med måleriets begränsade möjligheter att i disinkta färger och symboliskt abstrakta former återge mina upplevelser av dessa andliga giganter i teater och opera. Jag önskar att jag mer kunde öppna dörren till mitt inre och visualisera mina drömmar inför dem på ett vidare sätt än vad måleriet tillåter.

Kanske blir det i framtiden, genom teknikens under, möjligt att visualisera drömmar.

Momen

Erland Josephson

The Shakespearean tragedies of Karl Momen are no more illustrative of the characters which inspired them, than a fine Shakespearean actor's performance can be said to be a simple rendition of the play's script. A good actor does not illustrate, for that would result in failure. No matter how well considered or profound, such a performance would still lack the imaginative power, empathy, insight, and sense of fantasy that are all part of the finest actor's art, and its essential mystery. Without these elements the best actor's performance can be no more than a mere pastiche of the great playwright's incisive vision.

Momen is the artist painter as actor.
Within the self imposed rigor and internal order of his indefatigable style, there is an inherent and pervasive intonation that rises first to gesture, and then becomes at once interpretation and confession. The dynamic compositional elements of his paintings ebb and flow as their changing relationships reflect the timeless flux and transformative power of Shakespeare's masterful characterization of the human condition.

How does Momen identify with his subjects?
The actor who plays Macbeth, Richard III, and Henry V is one and the same person, and yet a metamorphosis occurs with each portrayal. So it is when Karl Momen "plays" the three roles. Half a shell, half man, the character is haunted by the conditions within the room in which he moves; the spectator is offered mutable variations of interpretation that are subtle and yet distinct.

What about the characters?
Perhaps, Momen is not concerned with characterization, but rather with the shaping of metaphor or symbol. His personalities have their destinies indelibly defined. They are hopelessly surrendered to a world in which they cling to their mistaken beliefs in an attempt to rise above their dire circumstances. They desperately want to step out of context, but the stage of life keeps them confined to its terrible and relentless design. Although they are unaware of their inevitable fate the spectator knows they are doomed. The armor, the magnificent armor, is empty. The helmet has holes for eyes; we feel their gaze but there is no encounter.

Hamlet is pulled deeper into the paradox as the shadow, and the one who casts the shadow, meld into one ominous figure. Formal and metaphysical contours are simultaneously established and dissolved as a simulacrum of the actor's mastery over time and space. Recurring emblems such as the crown and the bloodied sword portend the noblest aspirations coexisting with the menace of evil and destruction. Powerful characters are snared by their ambition. Motivated by false beliefs of their mastery over fate, they are crushed when their hopes are dashed. The rigorously executed paintings of Karl Momen traverse the marginal boundaries where discipline and human order are on the verge of catastrophic eruption, and disintegration. In the paintings inspired by Othello, Julius Cæsar, and Anthony and Cleopatra the emblematic has conquered. The characters are no longer visible. Behind signs, symbols, and monuments Cleopatra seems obliterated; she is hidden by her traces. Under the desert pyramids she slumbers in dreams of eternity; intangible, and inaccessible. The wreath that was to close around Cæsar's brow now encircles a void. The huge columns are like heavy portals opening towards oblivion, their imperious bearing lost forever, like temples that have forgotten their purpose.

Momen's paintings are decorative. Perhaps this is what holds them together, and the reason why they do not inspire abject despair in the viewer. As with Shakespeare, the form, the poetry, and the masterfully balanced cadence of profoundly evocative language, render the artist's insights bearable. Perhaps there is in Momen the hope that cruelties can be mitigated, and the desire for an alternative order which lies concealed beyond the grasp of our descriptive powers. These severe paintings reverberate with Momen's concern with essential humanism in the face of tragic abstraction.

Erland Josephson.

Swedish Translation:
Karl Momens bilder av några av Shakespeares karaktärer och skådespel är inte illustrationer, lika lite som skådespelares tolkningar och framställningar är det. Skådespelaren illustrerar inte, skulle så vara fallet är det fråga om ett misslyckande, möjligen en kommentar, kanske genomtänkt och djuplodande, men utan den inlevelse, fantasikänsla och identifikation som är skådespeleriets signum. Och mysterium.

MOMEN ÄR BILDKONSTNÄREN SOM SKÅDESPELARE.
Mitt i stramheten och den stränga ordningen förnimmer man starkt närvaron av en gest och ett tonfall, på en gång tolkning och bekännelse. Men hos Momen är också scenbilden i rörelse. Shakespeares ord sätter som alltid igång rastlösa förvandlingar, i människor, i tingen, i kunskapen.

HUR SER IDENTIFIKATIONEN UT?
Den skådespelare som gör Macbeth, Richard den tredje och Henrik den femte är en och samme person, samma kropp, samma ansikte. Och ändå en annan. Så också hos Momen när han "spelar" de tre rollerna. Halvt skal, halvt människa, jagad av de omständigheter som präglar rummet karaktärerna rör sig i, åskådaren erbjuds en serie variationer, återhållna men fullt märkbara.

KARAKTÄRERNA?
Kanske vill Momen inte alls "karaktärisera", snarare gestalta ett slags emblem, roller inskrivna i sina öden, hjälplöst utlämnade till en värld vars villkor de tror sig diktera. De vill liksom kliva ut ur bilden, men livets

scenografi binder dem. De vet det inte själva, men vi i publiken ser att de är dömda att gå under. Rustningen, den ståtliga rustningen, är tom. Hjälmen har hål för ögonen, vi känner en blick men möter den inte. Hamlet dras djupare in i den paradoxalt tydliga otydligheten, där skuggan och den som kastar skuggan liksom smälter samman i en enda gestalt. Konturerna är på en gång fasta och i upplösning, redan när det är en rolltolkning som står skådespelarens arbete nära. De återkommande emblemen, kronan och den blodröda svärdsklingan, rymmer både hot och önskedrömmar.

Maktmänniskorna är insnärjda i sina strävanden, de styrs av övertygelsen att de behärskar ödet, tills de krossas av insikten att detta var en illusion. Momens hårt disciplinerade bilder rör sig i de gränstrakter där all disciplin, all mänsklig ordning är på väg att sprängas sönder.

I bilderna kring Othello, Julius Cæsar och Antonius och Kleopatra har det emblematiska helt tagit över. Människan syns inte längre. Bakom tecken, symboler och monument tycks hon utplånad, hon döljs bakom sina spår. Under pyramiderna i öknen slumrar hennes evighetsdrömmar, ogripbara och förstenade. Kransen som skulle sluta sig kring Cæsars änne öppnar sig mot tomheten. De väldiga pelarna är som tunga portar ut mot glömskan, en bild av föroyckad högfärd, likt tempel som har förgätit sin innebörd.

Momens bilder är dekorativa, det är kanske det som håller dem samman, det är kanske på så sätt som de undgår att väcka åskådarens förtvivlan. Samma hos Shakespeare. Det är formen, poesin, det dekorativa språket som gör insikterna uthärdliga.

Kanske finns det också ett slags hopp om att grymheterna ska tämjas, en strävan mot en annan ordning, än så länge hemlighetsfull och svårbeskrivlig. I Momens stränga bilder vibrerar också en ton av protest mot människans försvinnande i emblem och heraldik.

Erland Josephson.

Homage to

William Shakespeare

HENRY V IS ONE OF SHAKESPEARE'S PLAYS that is a puzzle to me. As a prince, Henry was very interested in the theater and often participated in performances. He learned the ways of the common people. Devious pursuits such as cheating, trickery, and dishonesty were often learned from his friend Falstaff. Shakespeare was also an actor from a young age, this being one of his many interests throughout his life. It was during this era that actors were very much part of the common people and knew from personal experience how people thought, worked, and lived.

In Henry V the occupation of France is legitimized and celebrated with the marriage of princess Catherine of France. I find great difficulty in accepting this union in its masquerade of true love. Throughout history victors have taken not only their enemies' lands, but have also mingled their genes, through marriage with their vanquished foes. Two of the more dramatic examples are the marriage of Alexander he Great to Roxanne the Princess of Persia, and Caesar bringing Cleopatra to Rome as his consort, resulting in the birth of a son.

HENRY V.

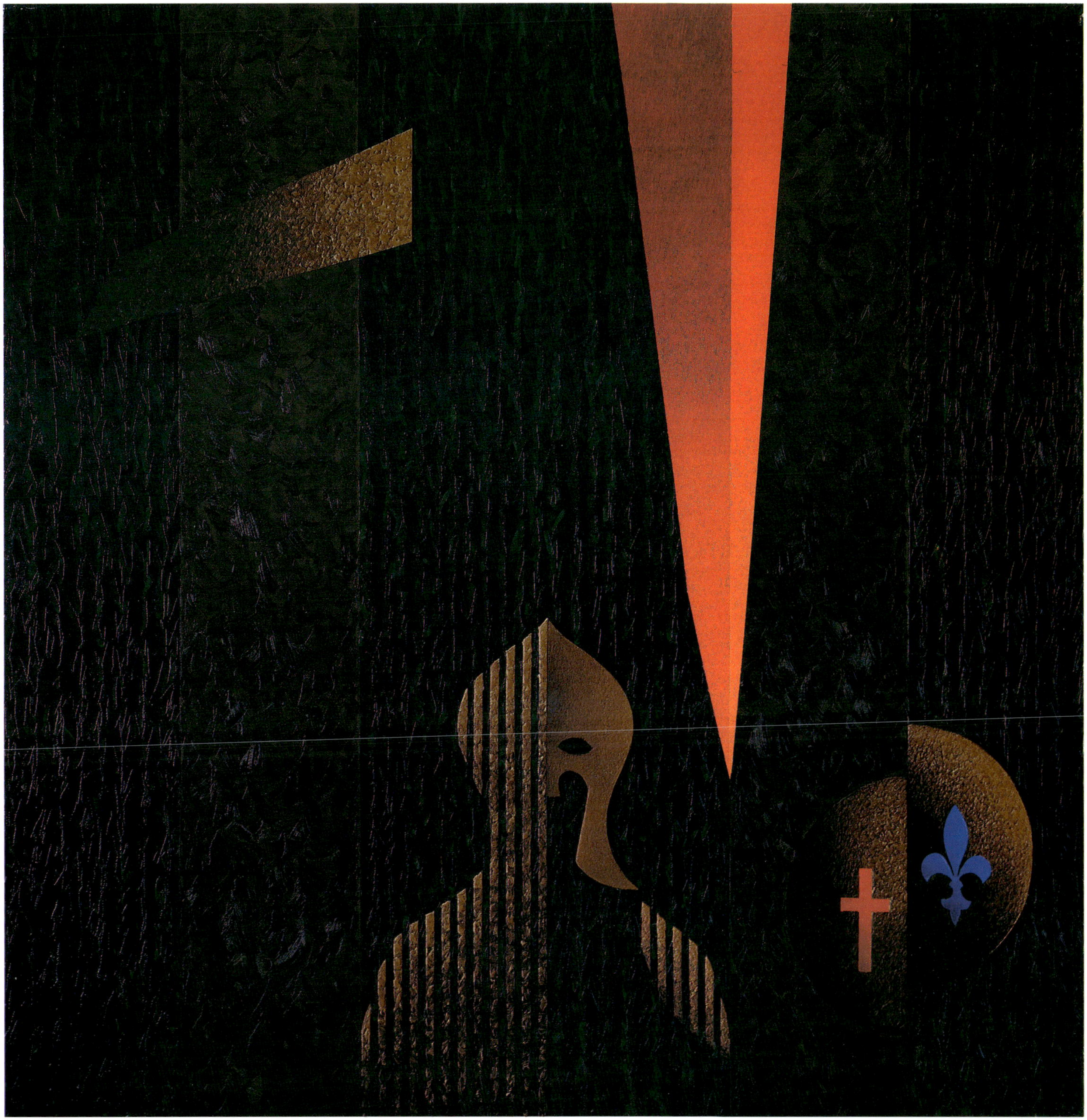

MY FIRST CONTACT WITH SHAKESPEARE was through a viewing of Sir Laurence Olivier's Richard III. Ironically, within a week of seeing this film I saw the first complete film documentary of the Third Reich. Barely a year after the Soviet occupation troops left my town. It was in 1949 or 1950, I think. For me the central question remains, What would have been Richard III's destiny if he had been physically well formed and a handsome young man? Would he still have become the evil and bloodthirsty tyrant of the play?

As an admirer of the great stoic philosopher Seneca, I wonder about mankind. Is the human condition solely determined by environmental factors, or by genes, or by both? This conundrum has received brilliant treatment by the 13th century Persian poet, Sa'di.

RICHARD III.

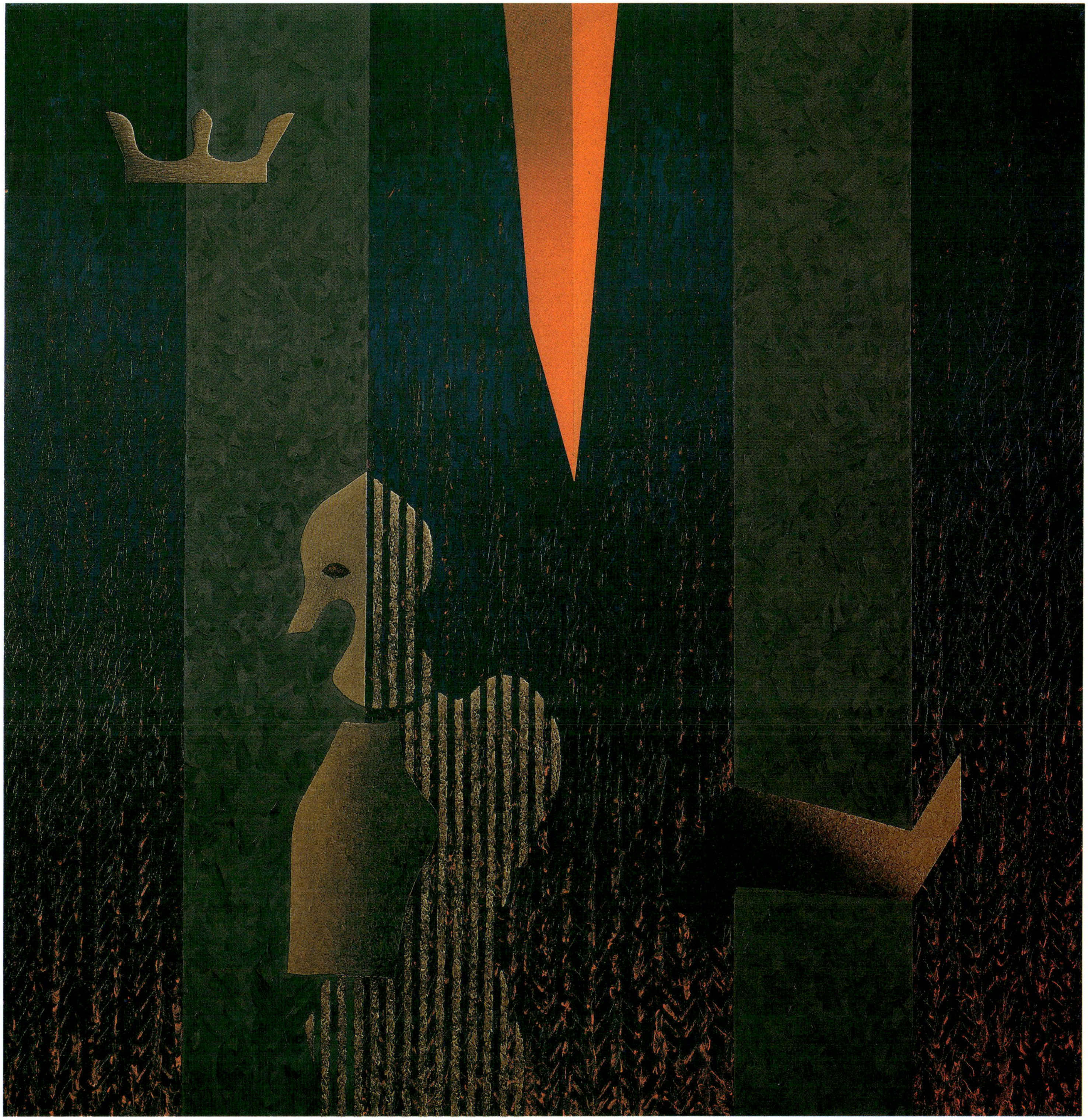

COMING FROM A COUNTRY AND FAMILY background where adherence to superstitious beliefs was the rule rather than the exception, I see the drama of Macbeth built on superstition and ambition as its major themes. Macbeth believed implicitly in the prediction of the witches that he would become king and that he would be killed "when Birnam Wood came to Dunsinane." He believed that he would be murderd by a man "who was not by mother born," namely Macduff, who came into the world by Caesarean section. When Macbeth was told of these events he refused to fight against Macduff as he could see no purpose in frustrating his predicated destiny. Consequently he was beheaded.

The second theme, that of ambition, is manifested in Lady Macbeth's desire to be queen. It was she who encouraged her husband to commit the evil act of murdering King Duncan. In the words of Moliere: "ambition les femmes inspire l'amour" – a phenomenon that has been repeated throughout history, from kings to peasants. A case in point is the last ruler of the Peacock Throne who was completely enslaved to superstitious and astrological beliefs. With dreams more anchored in utopia than in reality, he became indecisive and failed to act when he should have. Consequently, under the influence of his gentle but ambitious queen, he lost his kingdom. The lure of the supernatural has always appealed to those in high office. In 1597 King Jacob I of Scotland was so obsessed with witchcraft and magical powers that he wrote a book on witchcraft and demonology.

MACBETH.

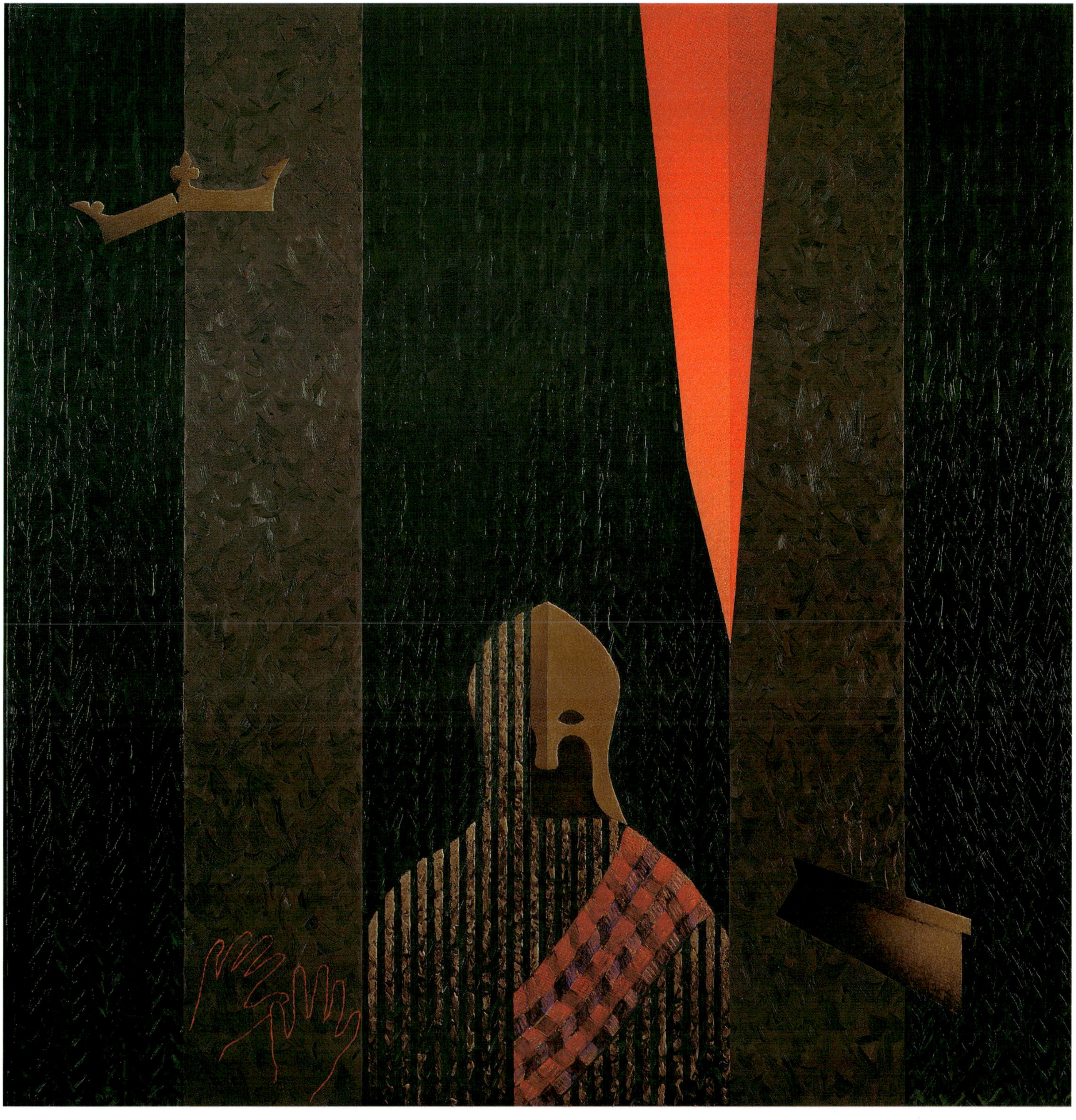

JULIUS CÆSAR IS ONE OF MY FAVORITE Shakespeare plays. Like an architect, Shakespeare has placed his compass and started to draw a circle that has circumscribed Cæsar's overruling of the senate, the plotting of the senators, and Cæsar's murder by the dagger of his best friend, Brutus. The highlight within this setting is the brilliant speech by Mark Anthony; the Romans rise up, the rebels are defeated, and the circle is completed when Mark Anthony is declared the new leader.

Every time I see Julius Cæsar performed I feel lost in a labyrinth with no exit. Cæsar is a military genius and democratic founder of the Roman Empire. I am confused in the thought that he also aspires to become a dictatorial ruler. This immediately brings to mind other generals, namely Napoleon and the "Kanzler" who perpetrated great disasters upon the world. There must be something in the make-up of many democratically elected rulers that leads them to believe that they own their nations. However, I acknowledge Cæsar's humanism and see him as one of the greatest founders of a democratic state, with great capacity for art and beauty.

JULIUS CÆSAR.

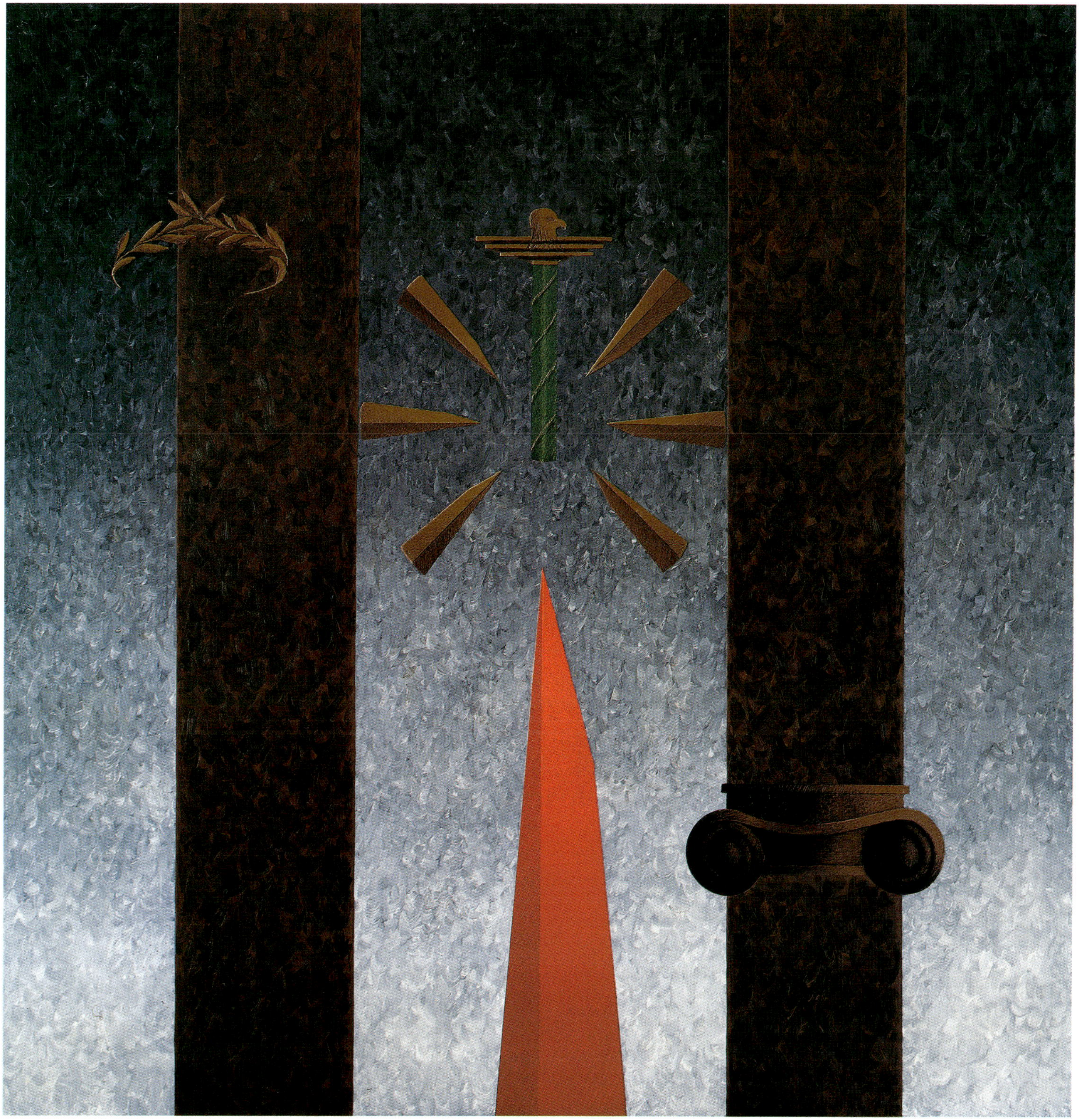

DURING THE SECOND PLAGUE in England, that lasted from April 1603 to March 1604, King Jacob I was unable to enter London for his coronation, and the English court was filled with uncertainty.

During the first years of King Jacob's rule London became an unpleasant place to live, especially for the ruling class. An air of pessimism prevailed. It was against this background that Shakespeare wrote a number of new plays which have come to be known as "problem plays." Anthony and Cleopatra, however, was the exception. In this play Shakespeare still accords charm and greatness to the central character, in preparation for his downfall. Shakespeare extends Greek and Roman mythology to the Egyptians and contradicts the historian view of Cleopatra (he saw Cleopatra as a wanton nymph) and allows her to give both her love and her life to Anthony.

ANTHONY AND CLEOPATRA.

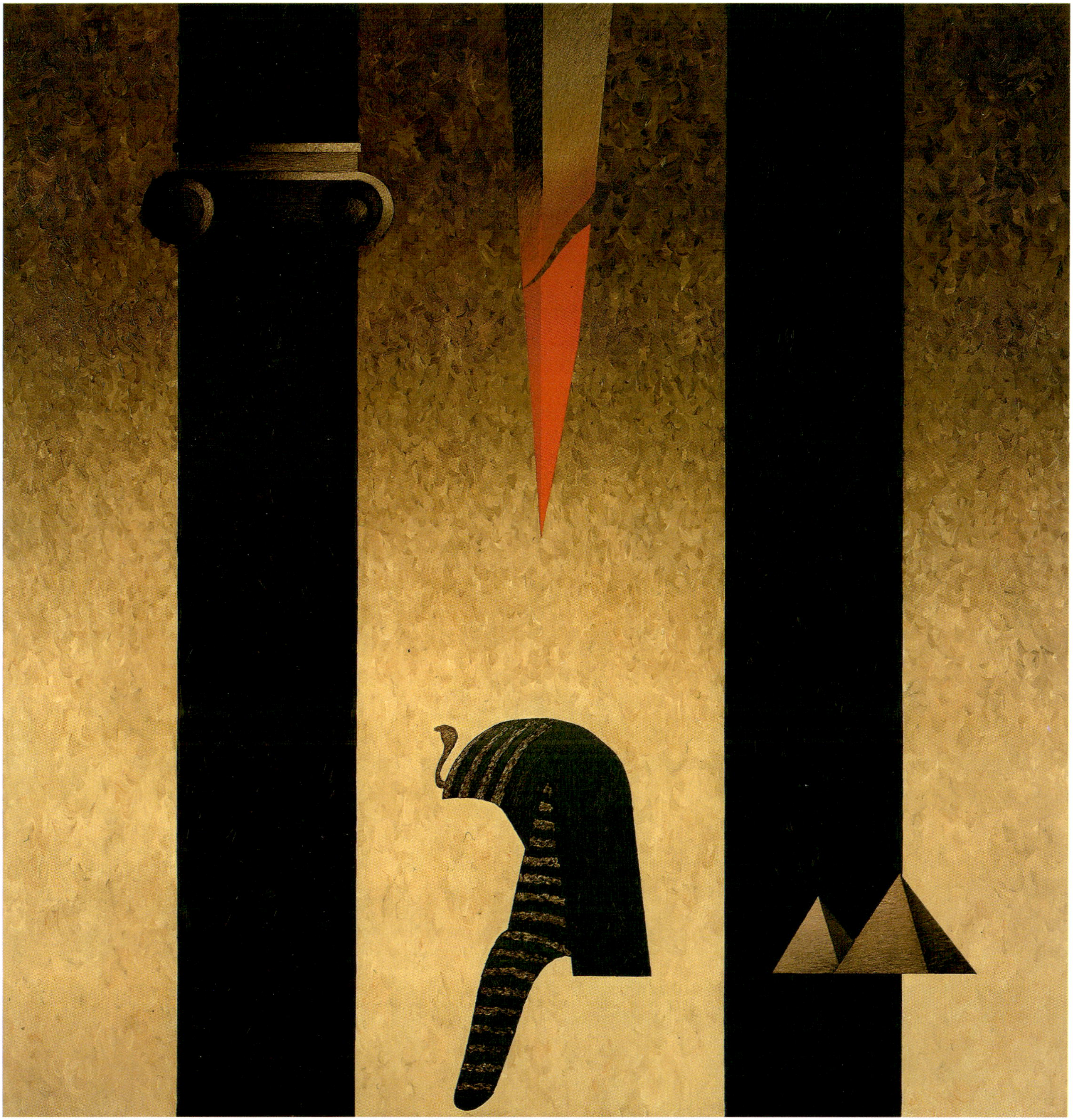

I FIND SHAKESPEARE MORE THAN A MASTER of language and drama. He is also a true diplomat, with skills that would hold their own in any modern political arena. He accorded the Moor the highest social status as general and Governor. However when it came to inter-racial marriage his attitude is not as definitive. Desdemona admitted to the Duke of Venice that her love for the Moor had been cemented during many years of listening to the tragic tales of the life and adventures of Othello. Her love was based more on pity and admiration than on impulsive and spontaneous passion.

In Verdi's opera Othello, Iago was cast as the most important character. This gave some critics in Milan reason to declare that Verdi should have named his opera "The Honest Iago"!

From my point of view, the drama begins when Othello grants rank promotion to Cassio instead of Iago. Iago later becomes the architect of the tragic events that bring the play to its bitter end.

OTHELLO.

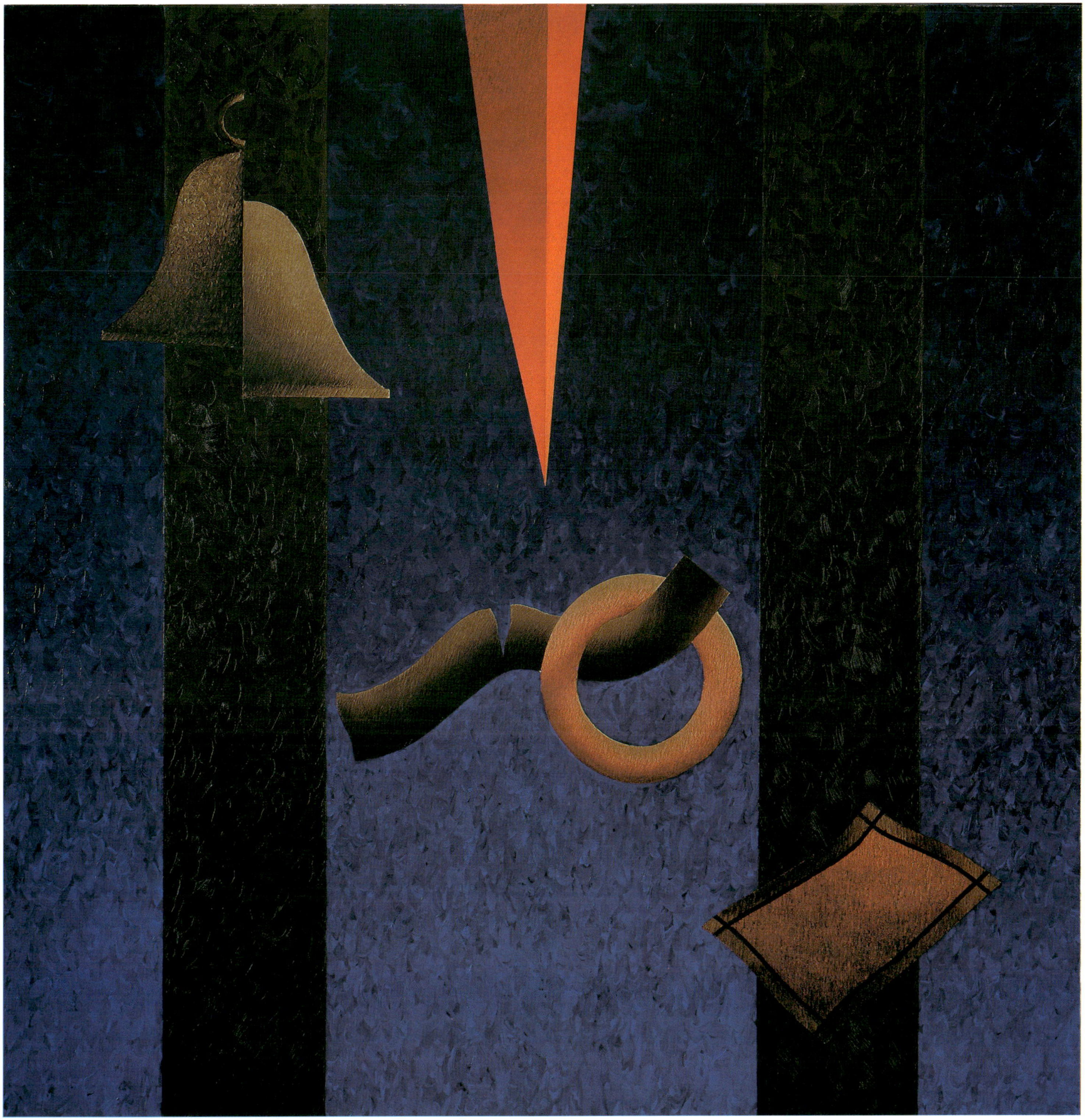

KNOWING THAT SHAKESPEARE HAD A SON, Hamnet, who died at the age of twelve in the plague of 1596, I wonder if this tragic event had something to do with the tragic ending of Romeo and Juliet. In the play the letter from Friar Lawrence informing Romeo that Juliet is not dead but merely in deep sleep, never arrives due to the quarantine order that seals the messenger within the guest house. As Romeo does not receive this fateful message he resolves to take his own life in one of the saddest and most tragic death scenes in Shakespearian drama.

In Romeo and Juliet I feel the hate and aversion that Shakespeare had for family fueds and, on a larger scale, for the wars between nations.

I wonder why Shakespeare has always characterized the nurse as truly caring and loving. She understands best how to love and nurture those in her care, whereas the parents are often preoccupied with financial concerns and with providing material comforts. I see Romeo and Juliet as one of the finest masterpieces of Shakespeare's genius. In this work he confronts comedy and tragedy simultaneously.

ROMEO AND JULIET.

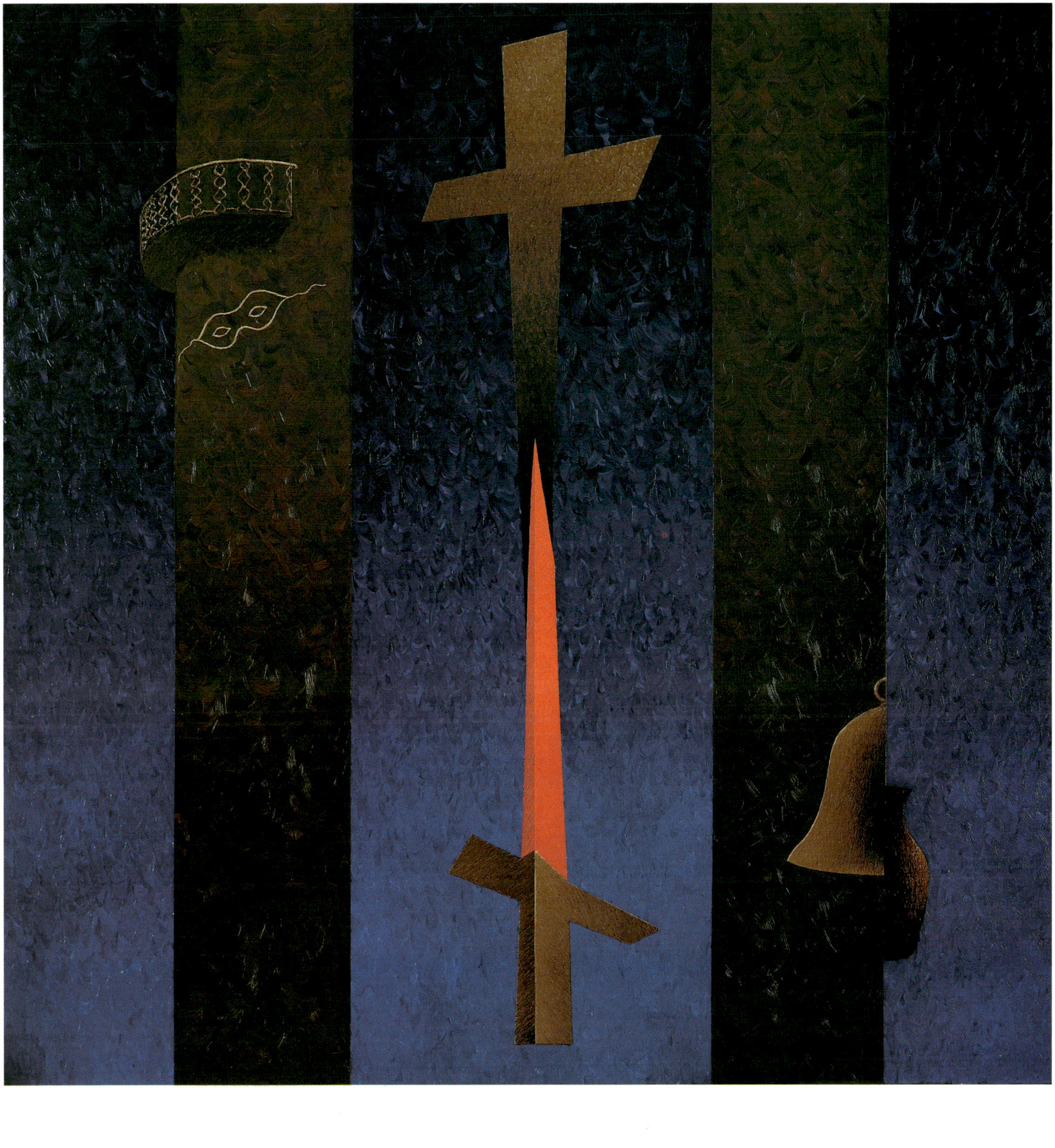

HAMLET IS FOR ME THE MOST COMPLEX of Shakespeare's plays. The first production of Hamlet that I saw was performed by Sir Laurence Olivier. But it was in July 1969 that I first visualized the entire play. All day long I walked about Kronborg Castle in Helsingör. I saw the traveling theater company performing in the reception hall of the castle. I visualized the king and queen in their confusion and embarrassment at seeing a reenactment of their own tragic act; with Hamlet observing them, all the while, as he planned his revenge. I saw the stabbed body of Ophelia's father behind the curtain in the queen's chamber, and outside the castle, Ophelia's empty grave with the bishop refusing to grant her a Christian burial because she died no longer a virgin.

In the final act I saw the large hall; the dying Hamlet throwing the poisoned sword through the air. I saw the sword piercing the king's back. Then I awoke from my daydreams with the taste of ambition, adultery, thievery, revenge, and murder still in my mouth.

HAMLET.

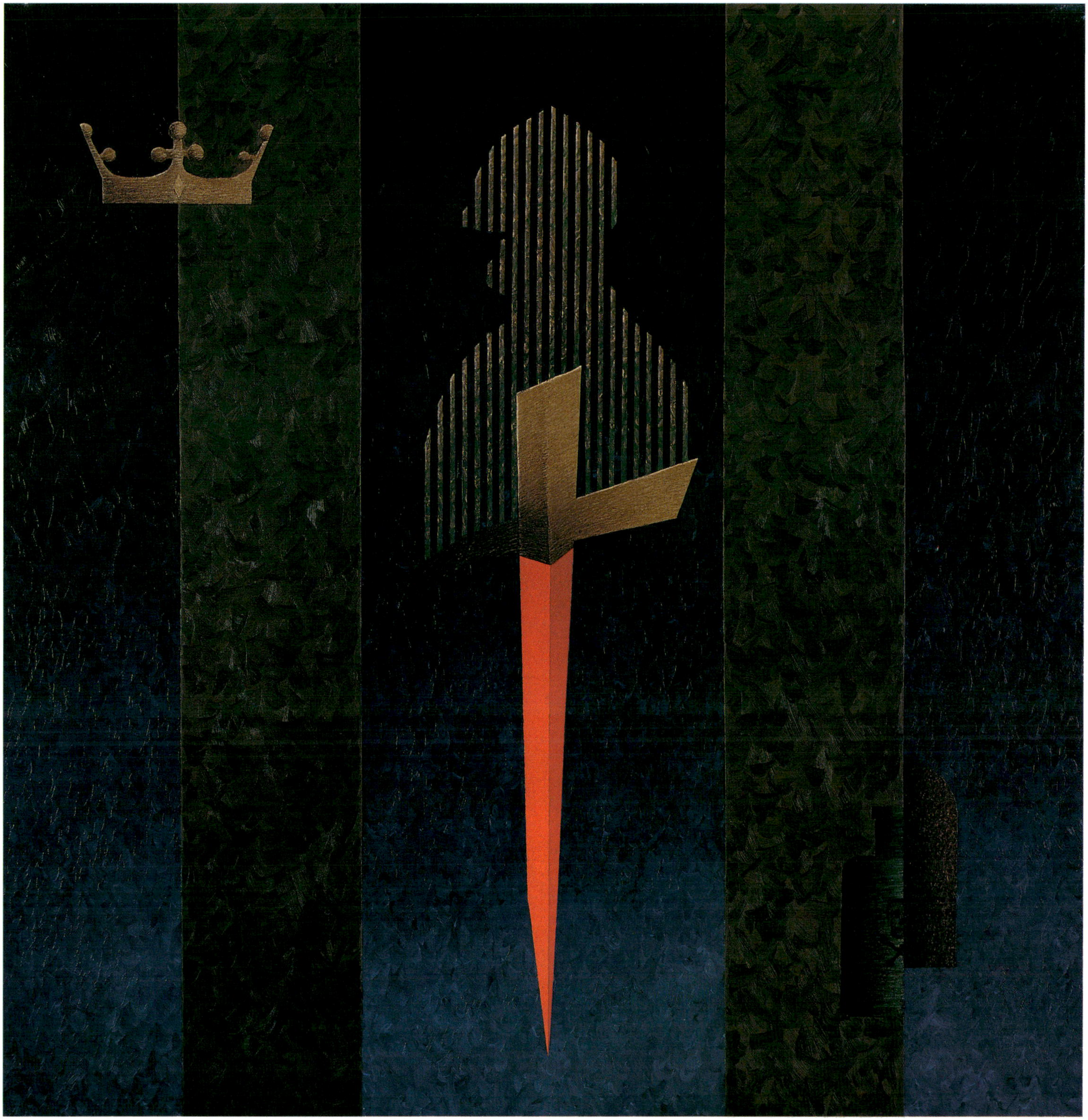

Homage to

Richard Wagner

James A. Mason

It seems appropriate for Karl Momen to interpret Richard Wagner's music dramas into his own art form. He is not only a devotee of Wagner but like the composer his understanding and interest go beyond his own art. He is well travelled and well read. Both Wagner and Momen have been influenced by not only art and music but by literature, drama, and even political and moral issues.

Where Wagner was a master of orchestral color with few equals, the same claim can be made about Momen's use of enlivened subtle gradations of color, vibrant hues, and textures. Wagner's emotional fervor and luxuriant resources of harmony and color in *Tannhäuser* are achieved in Momen's depictions through his use of dynamic color in the painting of various symbolic suggestions that are found in Wagner's music dramas.

Wagner held his works together with recurring concise themes or "leitmotifs" that were varied and developed throughout his music. Momen uses geometric elements such as spheres, cubes, and cones in a similar way for their symbolic and unifying value.

The nordic myths used in developing the librettos for the cycle of music dramas called *The Ring of the Niebelung* offered opportunities for effective theater but they also embodied a concentrated, poetic quality and certain philosphical issues that were important to Wagner in the way he perceived human life. In looking at Momen's depiction of *Das Rheingold, Die Walküre, Siegfried,* and *Götterdämmerung* the same opportunities found in the music dramas become prominent through appropriate symbols such as the sword, the helmet, the spear, the cross, the cup and numerous other objects.

Wagner was the last great figure of German romanticism. Romantic opera culminated with his *Lohengrin.* In *Lohengrin* and *Der Fliegende Holländer*, Momen departs from his characteristic geometric abstraction to depict a ghostly swan growing ominously from the water. The cathedral in this painting is represented in an etherial, almost other worldly, manner—all in keeping with the romantic tradition. The character of Friedrich von Telramound suffers split loyalties between his chivalric honor and coming to the aid of his wife in her ambitious desires to become the countess of Brabant. In *Der Fliegende Holländer* Momen majestically represents the trauma and melancholy of a sinking ship in search of redemption while anchored to the reality of true love.

Wagner's last work was *Parsifal* which has been described as a consecration festival drama based on the legend of the holy grail. It could not become the drama of the Christian redemption but rather an artistic substitute for religion, which Wagner believed he could represent by pure ethics within the context of a religious aura. In Momen's painting for *Parsifal* he presents the cross in a reverential manner. The cross is the focus of the composition and has the sanctity of a Good Friday. Momen depicts with brilliance the purity and light of the holy grail, symbolizing all of humanity's metaphysical beliefs.

Wagner asserted that the artist should use his ability to influence culture, to elevate and educate people through art. He changes the direction of tonality in music for future composers with his complex chromatic alterations of chords in *Tristan*. His constant shifting of key and the blurring of progression with non-harmonic tones became an identifying landmark in music. Momen's cool metallic colors, patterned brush strokes, and dynamic spatial achievements represent the work of another artist in his search for a noble and spiritual dimension in his craft.

James A. Mason

Swedish translation:

Det förefaller naturligt för Karl Momen att tolka Richard Wagners musik i sitt eget konstnärliga uttryckssätt. Karl Momen är inte bara en hängiven Wagnerian utan som kompositören sträcker sig hans intressen och insikter långt bortom den egna konsten. Han är berest och bildad. Både Wagner och Momen har låtit sig påverkas inte bara av konsten och musiken utan också av litteraturen, teatern, ja till och med av politiska och moraliska frågor. Wagner var en mästare utan like i sin förmåga att orkestrera klangfärger. Detsamma kan sägas om Momens förmåga att ge liv åt subtila färgskalor, vibrerande skiftningar och strukturer. Den känslomässiga glöden och de ymniga källorna av harmonier och färger i Wagners Tannhäuser motsvaras av Momens framställningar där han målar i dynamiska färger som skapar en symbolik vilken återfinns i Wagners musik och drama.

Wagner knöt ihop sina arbeten med stöd av återkommande sammanhållna teman, leitmotifs, som varieras och utvecklas genomgående i musiken. Momen använder geometriska element såsom klot, kuber och koner på ett liknande sätt i deras egenskap av symboler och sammanhållande värden.

De nordiska gudasagor som använts för att utveckla libretton i den musikaliska dramacykeln Niebelungens Ring erbjöd möjligheter för verkningsfull teater. Men de förkroppsligade även koncentrerad poetisk kvalitet och filosofiska föreställningar som var viktiga för Wagner och hur han uppfattade mänskligt liv. När vi ser Momens bilder av Das Rheingold, Die Walküre, Siegfried och Götterdämmerung framstår möjligheterna på samma sätt som i de musikaliska dramerna genom träffande symboler som svärdet, hjälmen, spjutet, korset, kalken och ett antal andra objekt.

Wagner var den siste av en rad viktiga personer i den tyska romantiken. Lohengrin var kulmen på den romantiska operan. I Lohengrin och Den Flygande Holländaren gör Momen avsteg från den annars karakteristiska geometriska abstraktionen genom skildringen av en spöklik svan som olycksbådande växer ur vattnet. Katedralen i denna målning uttrycks på ett eteriskt, nästan utomjordiskt manér – allt i enlighet med den romantiska traditionen. Friedrich von Telramounds karaktär lider av motstridiga lojalitetskrav mellan riddarens ära och stödet för hustruns ambition att bli hertiginna av Brabant. I den Flygande Holländaren beskriver Momen majestätiskt det sjunkande skeppets trauma och melankoli i sitt sökande efter förlossning samtidigt som det är fast förankrat i den sanna kärlekens realitet.

Wagners sista verk Parsifal har beskrivits som ett helgelse-drama på basis av legenden om den heliga graal. Det kunde aldrig bli ett drama om den kristna förlossningen utan snarare ett konstnärligt substitut för religion som Wagner trodde han kunde beskriva genom en rent etisk framställning omgiven av en religiös atmosfär. Momen presenterar ett kors i målningen Parsifal på ett vördnads-fullt sätt. Korset utgör focus i konstverket som har en djup fromhet. Momen beskriver briljant renheten och ljuset hos den heliga graal, symboliserande alla mänskliga meta-fysiska trossatser.

Wagner slog fast att konstnären var förpliktad att an-vända sin förmåga att göra intryck på kulturen och att upphöja och utbilda människor genom konsten. Han förändrade inriktningen för musikens tonalitet och på-verkade framtidens kompositörer genom sina komplexa kromatiska ändringar i ackorden i Tristan. Den ständigt pågående skiftningen av tonart och blandningen av pro-gressioner med icke harmoniska toner blev en milstolpe i musikens historia. Momens svala metalliska färgsättning, mönstrade penseldrag och dynamiska rumsliga företräden representerar arbete av en annan konstnär i sökandet efter en ädel och andlig dimension i sitt konstnärskap.

James A. Mason

IN SHAPING HIS *RING OF THE NIBELUNG*, Wagner delved deep into Teutonic myth and legend for his drama of Siegfried and the fall of the pagan gods led by Wotan, or Odin. As the Siegfried story was passed down from generation to generation, it came to embrace the real life exploits of Attila and the Huns. A century after Attila's death in 453 A.D., the legend gradually split into two versions, the German and the Scandinavian. The German, called the *Nibelungenlied,* was written down in the 12th century. It emphasized history over myth and gave the legend a Christian frame of reference. Scandinavian versions emerged in the Icelandic *Eddas* and two Norse sagas, the 12th century Volsunga Saga and the 13th century Thidrek Saga, both which retained more of the legend's primitive, supernatural aspects.

When writing the *Ring*, Wagner turned principally to the Eddas and Sagas, for in them he found the majesty and sense of Fate that he wished to convey in his own work. While he synthesized the sagas and made some significant changes in plot and character, he retained many details common to all, such as the use of the dragon's blood which enables Siegfried to understand the language of the birds. The charts by *Die Walküre,* on next double spread, illustrates the variations in the geneaology of the principal characters of the Siegfried legend in the two Norse sagas, the *Nibelungenlied, and* Wagners *Ring.* The names vary only slightly from version to version, with the exeption of Attila who is Etzel in the *Nibelungenlied.*

DAS RHEINGOLD.

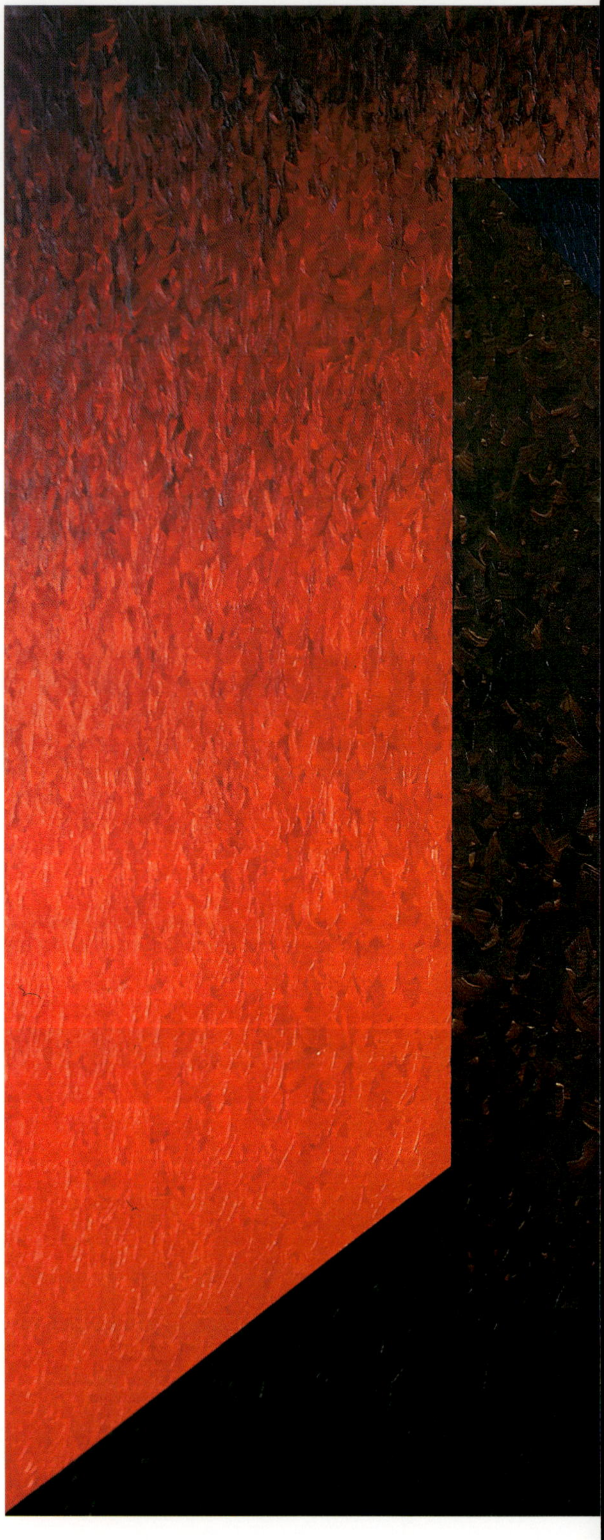

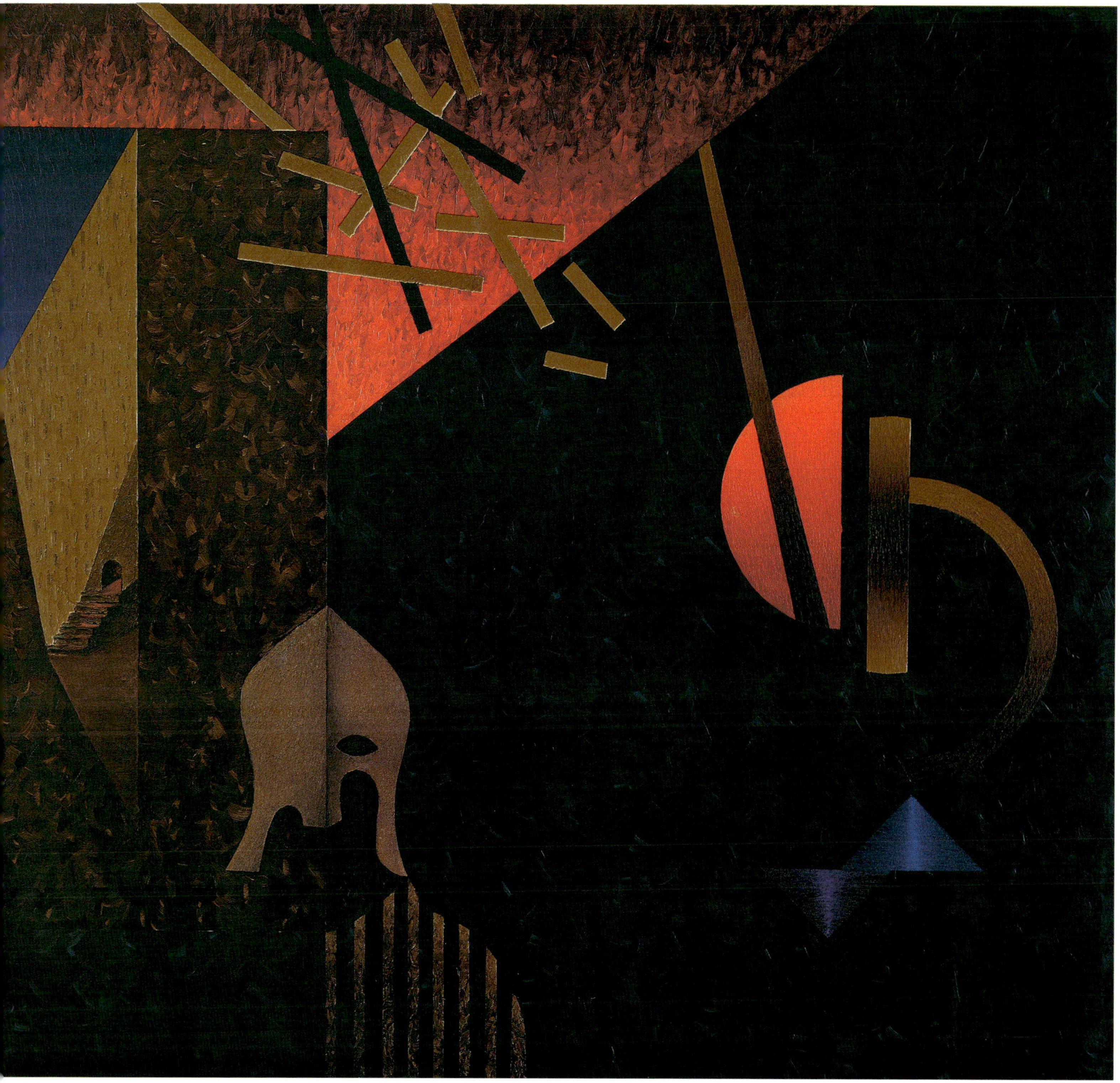

VOLSUNGA SAGA

Odin

Sigmund, married to *Hjordis* and twin of *Signy*

Sigurd, married to *Gudrune*

THIDREK SAGA

Sigmund *Aldrian*, married to *Ode*

Sigfrid, married to;

1. Brynhild,

2. Grimhild, sister of *Gunther* and *Hagen* (Odes son with an elf)
she was later married to *Attila*

NIBELUNGENLIED

Siegmund, twin of *Sieglinde*

Siegfried, married to

Kriemhild, sister of *Gunther* who was married to *Brunhilde*
she was later married to *Etzel* (Attila)
Hagen was her vassal

RING OF THE NIBELUNG

Wotan

Siegmund, twin of *Sieglinde* (married to Hunding), and brother of *Brunnhilde*

Siegfried, married to; *Alberich* brother of *Mime*

1. Brunnhilde, later married to Gunther

2. Gutrune, sister of *Gunther* who was half brother of *Hagen*, son of *Alberich*

DIE WALKÜRE.

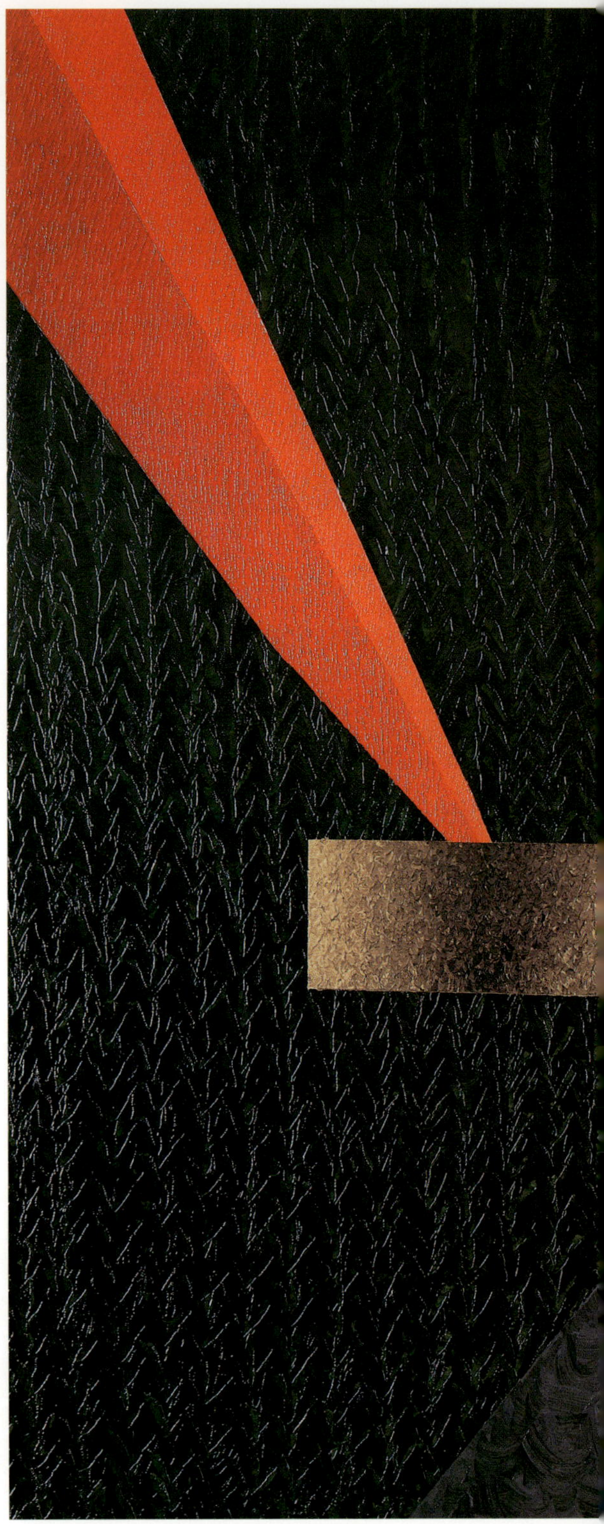

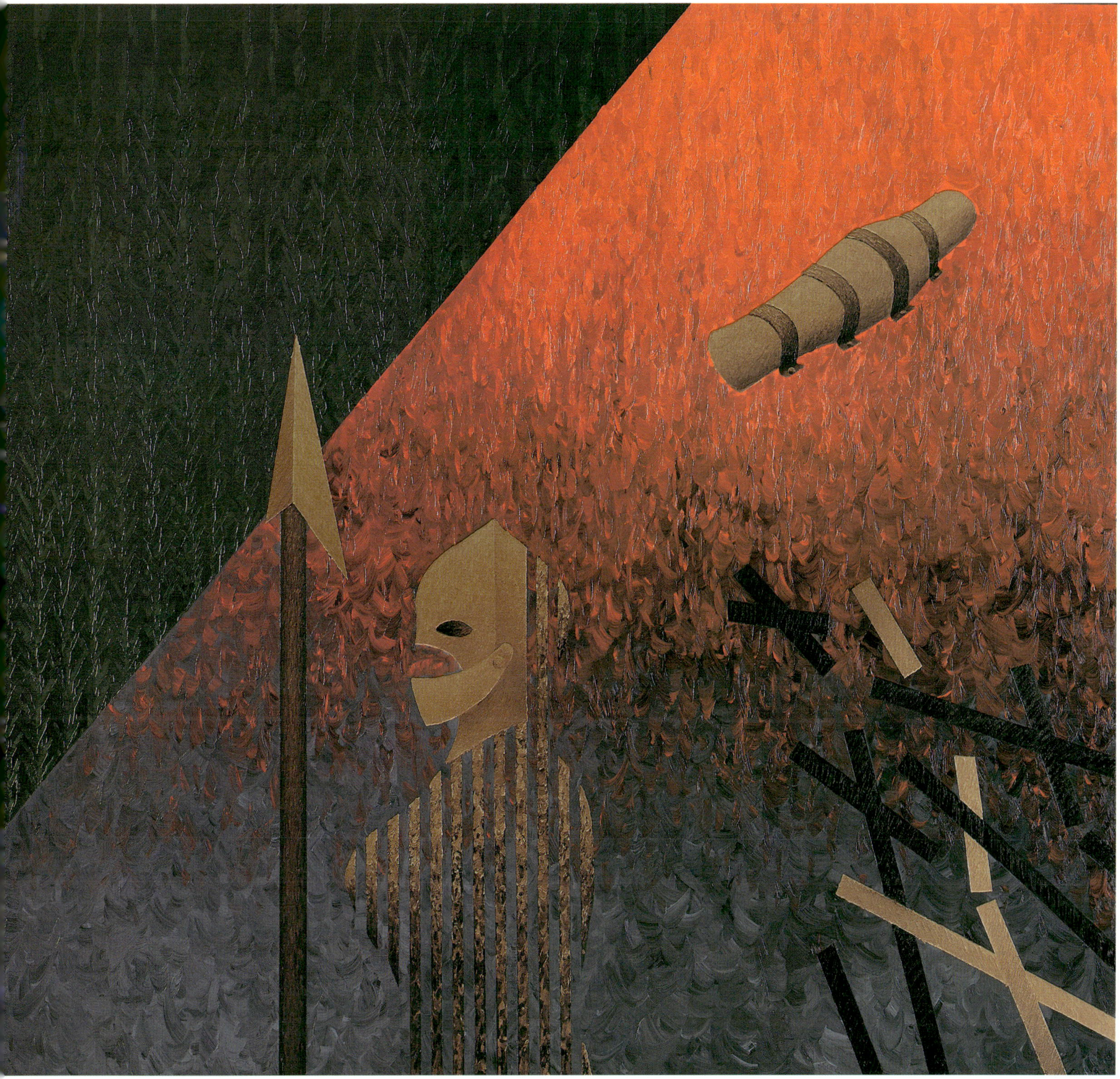

WHEN NIETZSCHE VISITED WAGNER for the first time in Triebschen on the Lake of Lucerne, he waited a lengthy while on his doorstep before knocking. He could hear the sound of a piano from within, as Wagner played Brunhilde's complaint from Siegfried the opera. Only when Wagner came to a break was Nietzsche shown in. Ironically, it was only after he had heard and discussed *Der Ring des Nibelungen* with Wagner, that same night, that Nietzsche formed the concept for one of his most important works *Die Geburt der Tragödie* (1870-71), one of the cornerstones of Nietzsche's atheist philosophy.

It was at four o'clock on a Sunday morning in June, 1869, that Cosima gave birth to Siegfried, and it was at the same day that Wagner completed the composition of his opera Siegfried. Nietzsche, who was staying with the Wagner family at the time, did not know about this event. Wagner later wrote to a friend that it was coincidental that on that day two Siegfrieds were born, however, only one was going to be immortal, referring to the opera.

SIEGFRIED.

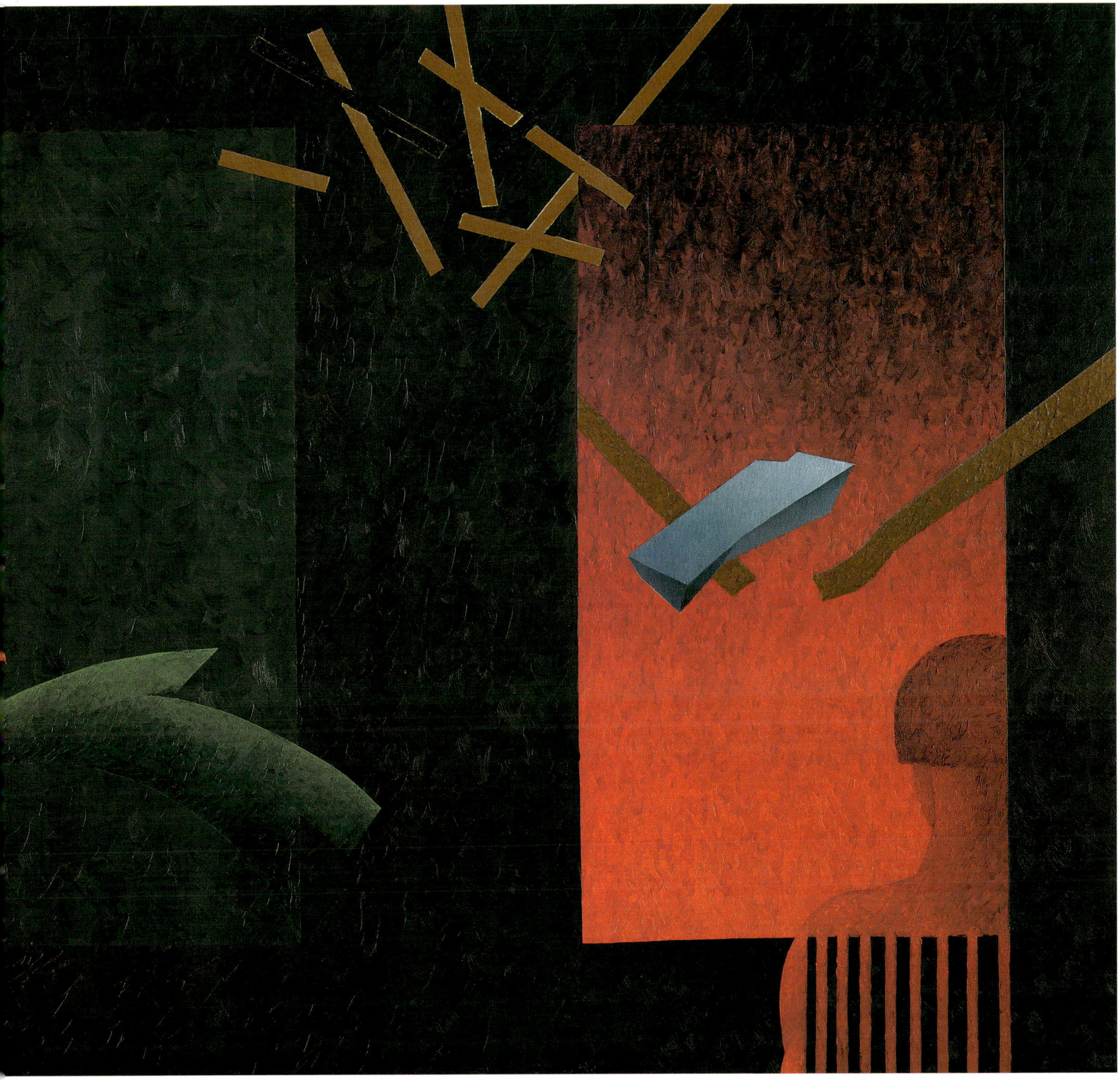

AGAINST OTHER POPULAR CONTENDERS George Bernard Shaw set up Richard Wagner as his own personal champion. To be with Wagner was for him to be with progress; he admired Wagner enormously. Shaw published his book *The Perfect Wagnerite* in 1898. In this work he interpreted the Ring as a condemnation of the capitalist system, in their turn he saw the Niebelungs as the ill-treated working class, the giants as skilled artisans, Alberich as an incompetent captain of industry, and Wotan, and the other gods as the privileged ruling classes. Siegfried is represented as the young Fabian, born to save the world.

Shaw took Wagner to task for not allowing Siegfried and Brunhilde, in the Götterdämmerung, to dedicate themselves to the benefit of humankind; instead they settled for the trivial satisfaction of romantic love, "the love panacea" as Shaw contemptuously refered to it.

Wagner began to write the Ring as a future revolutionary, with a price on his head, while living in conservative Prussia. However, the enthusiasm that Shaw had for the composer of Tristan and Isolde is puzzling, and cannot merely be explained on the grounds of Marxism or parallelism.

Whatever the reasons for Shaw's liking for Wagner, *The Perfect Wagnerite* is one of Shaw's most characteristic and inspirational works, filled with good humor and much laughter.

GÖTTERDÄMMERUNG.

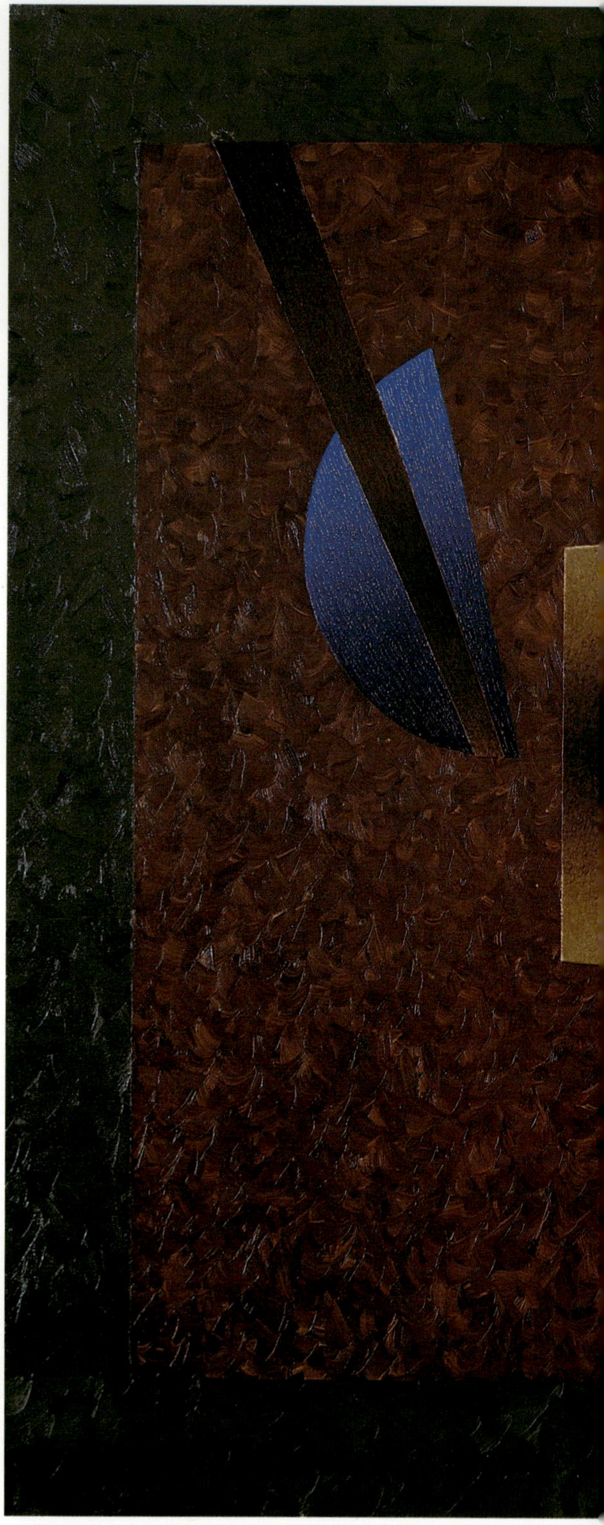

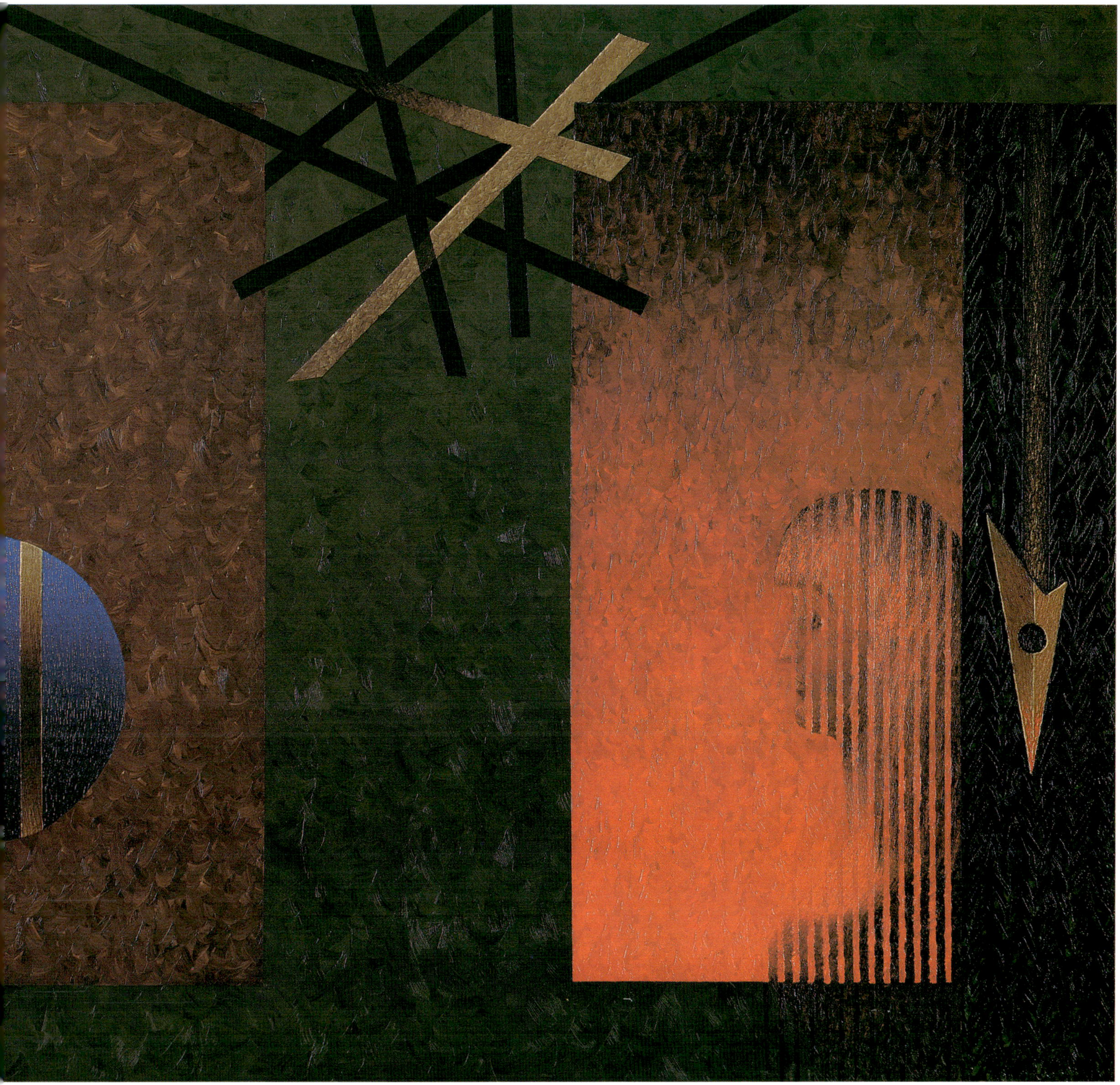

WAGNER'S NOTORIOUS INVOLVEMENT in the Dresden uprising did not endear him to the court. At the start of their friendship King Ludwig of Bavaria had asked Wagner to define his political views. The result was the July 1864 essay *On the State and Religion* which Ludwig heartily agreed with. In an earlier essay Wagner hailed the king as a superman, the representative of the "purely human." Ludwig had been assured that Wagner would never descend to the level of common politics and that he had been mistakenly branded a revolutionary by deficient intelligence police who judge only from outward appearance. Under the influence of Cosima, Wagner repressed his socialistic and revolutionary ideas and progressively became a "racist." In Lohengrin Wagner saw the highest German ideals.

In Lohengrin Wagner was deeply involved with the acting which he called, "Lohengrin ein Bühnenspiel." Here the difference between Nietzsche and Wagner was clear. Nietzsche wrote, "For complete relaxation of thought I need music. And what have I to do with drama, with the fighter and the spicy ecstasy of hocus pocus? I am anti-theatrical, but Wagner to the contrary is an enthusiastic theater man."

LOHENGRIN.

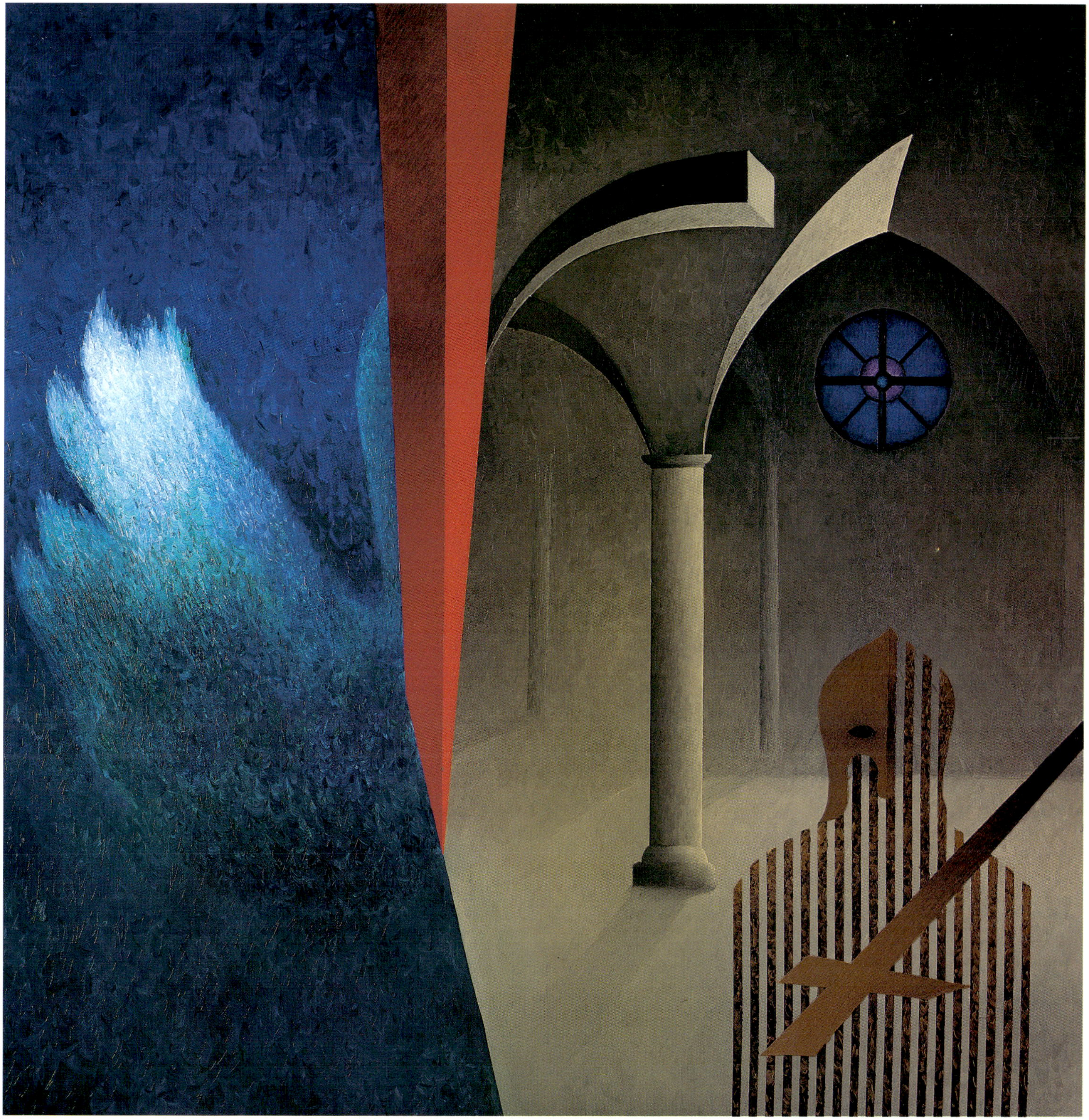

As an adherent of Schopenhauer's pessimistic philosophy, Wagner wrote to Frans Liszt stating, "in my thoughts I have sketched one Tristan and Isolde, the most simple and most honest musical concept with a black flag, with which I would cover myself and die."

Wagner dramatically changed the mythical Celtic tale. In the original tale Tristan was portrayed as the nephew of King Mark of Cornwall. In a duel he kills Morholt, brother of the Irish Queen and the uncle of Iseult. At a court feast King Mark displayed a long fair hair and proclaimed that he would marry no other than its owner. Tristan promises to find the owner of the hair.

In the Celtic tale, Tristan and Iseult fall in love and spend months wandering around in remorse before Iseult returns to King Mark. She feels great loyalty to the King, and Tristan is forced to flee to Britanny. There he weds Iseult to the White Hand "for her name and her beauty," but makes her his wife in name only. When Tristan is wounded in battle he sends for Iseult to come and heal him. If she accedes to his request the ship on which she embarks is to have a white sail, if she refuses, it is to be black. Motivated by jealousy, Tristan's wife informs him that the ship on which Iseult is hastening to her lover's aid is carrying a black sail. On hearing this news Tristan dies and Iseult, arriving too late to save her lover, yields up her life in a final embrace.

When Toscanini was a young student of composition, he decided after having seen *Tristan and Isolde*, that he would give up composing and only become a conductor. He later became one of the foremost interpreters of Wagner's works.

Even Puccini stopped composing for a while after seeing *Tristan and Isolde*. During this period his friends would hear him instead, humming the love duet of *Tristan and Isolde*.

Tristan und Isolde.

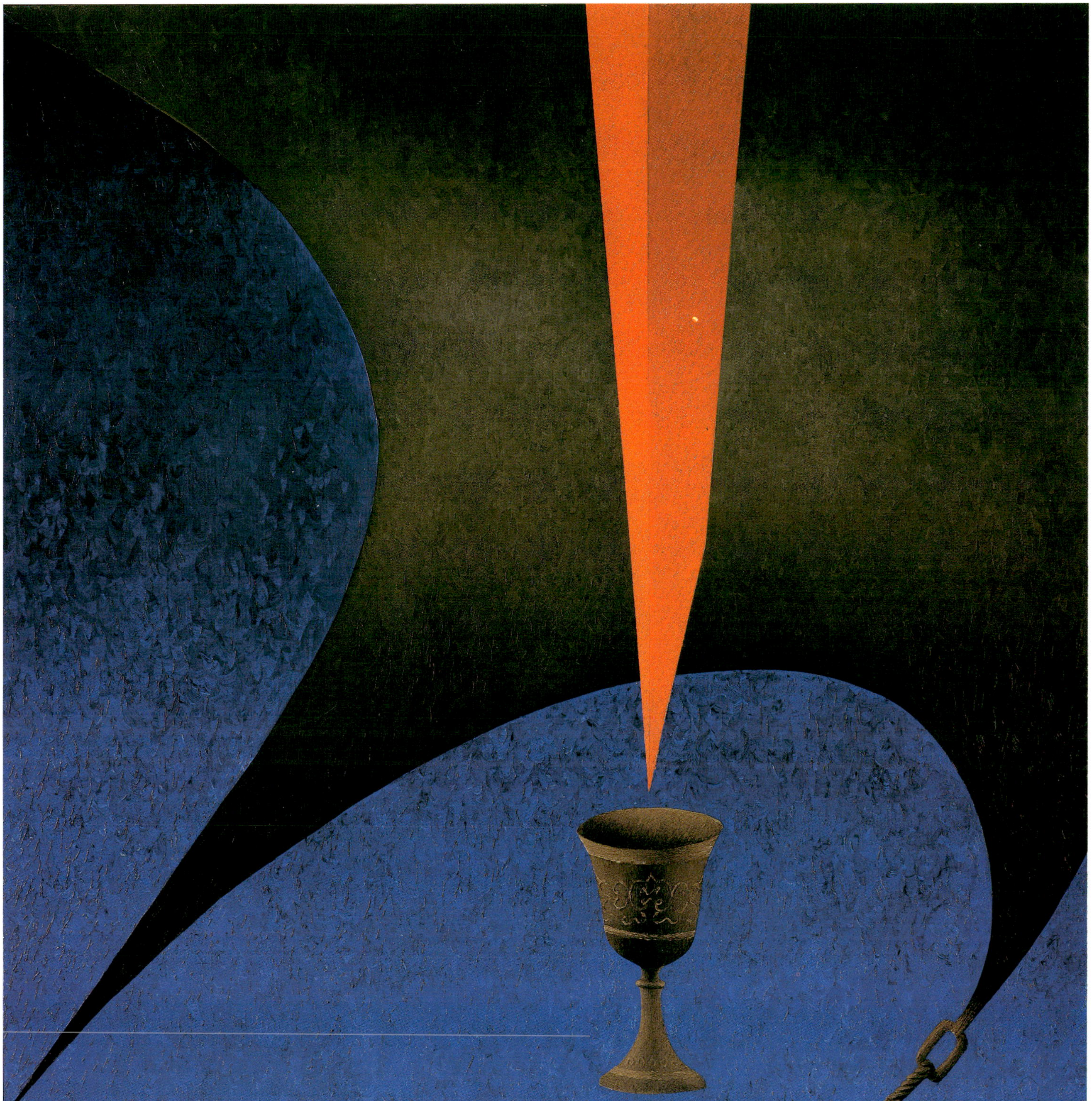

In July 1839 Richard and Minna Wagner, accompanied by their pet dog Robber, eluded Cossack boarder guards and waiting creditors to board a small Prussian trading vessel, the Thetis. After crawling through thick wet grass they were smuggled aboard the 106 ton vessel by Captain Wulff, without passports and bereft of their possessions. Wagner and his wife then endured the final humiliation of having to hide among the cargo for hours until the official inspection was completed and Thetis could sail from the little village outside Riga, into the Baltic Sea toward freedom.

Once at sea, the ship encountered a violent storm. The agonizing seasickness, sleeplessness, and boredom within the confines of their cramped quarters, attuned Wagner's sensibilities to the familiar tale of the Flying Dutchman that was recounted by the superstitious seamen. Throughout his life Wagner had searched for a woman who would be willing to give her life for him; this desire found expression in Elsa von Brabant, in *Lohengrin* and Isolde in *Tristan and Isolde.*

Der Fliegende Holländer.

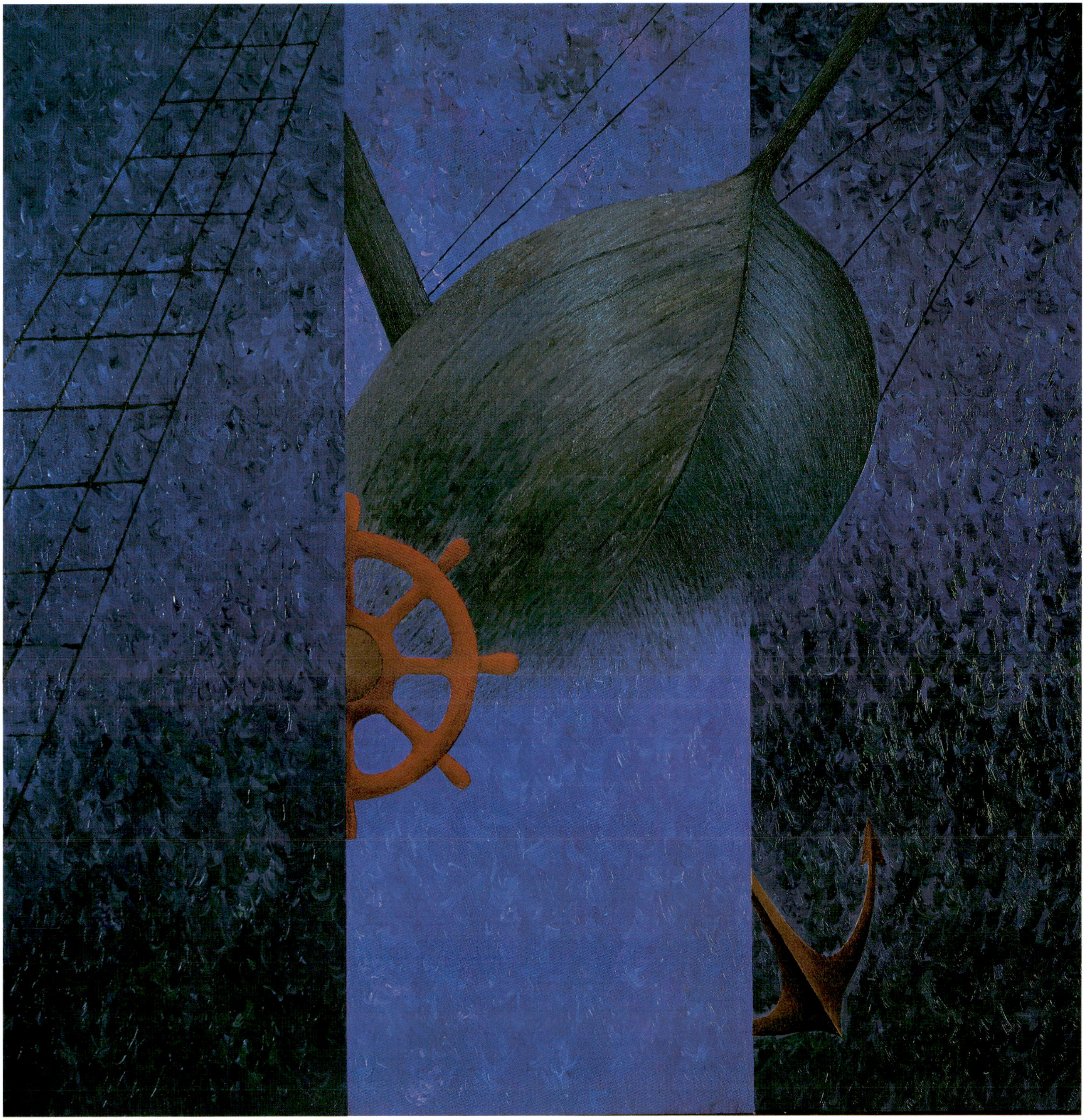

DIE MEISTERSINGER VON NÜRENBERG WAS directly related to German history and was the only comedy of all of Wagner's operas. With regard to Wagner and Cosima's rather complicated ethnic backgrounds, I keep Wagner the composer apart from Wagner the man with Germanic ideas. The more I read about Wagner the more I find that there are more questions than answers. Wagner had an extreme dislike for bureaucrats, accountants, and bankers; a sentiment not unexpected in a man with such a miserable history of failed financial affairs, something which also affected many other composers, artists, and authors throughout the history, and of course it is not a novelty for myself either. His aversion found expression in his characterization of Beckmesser. Notwithstanding his liberal socialistic ideas, Wagner nurtured an extreme admiration for the aristocracy, an idealization which he personified in the character of Walter von Stoltzing. Wagner concludes the opera with a defense of the purity of German art.

DIE MEISTERSINGER VON NÜRENBERG.

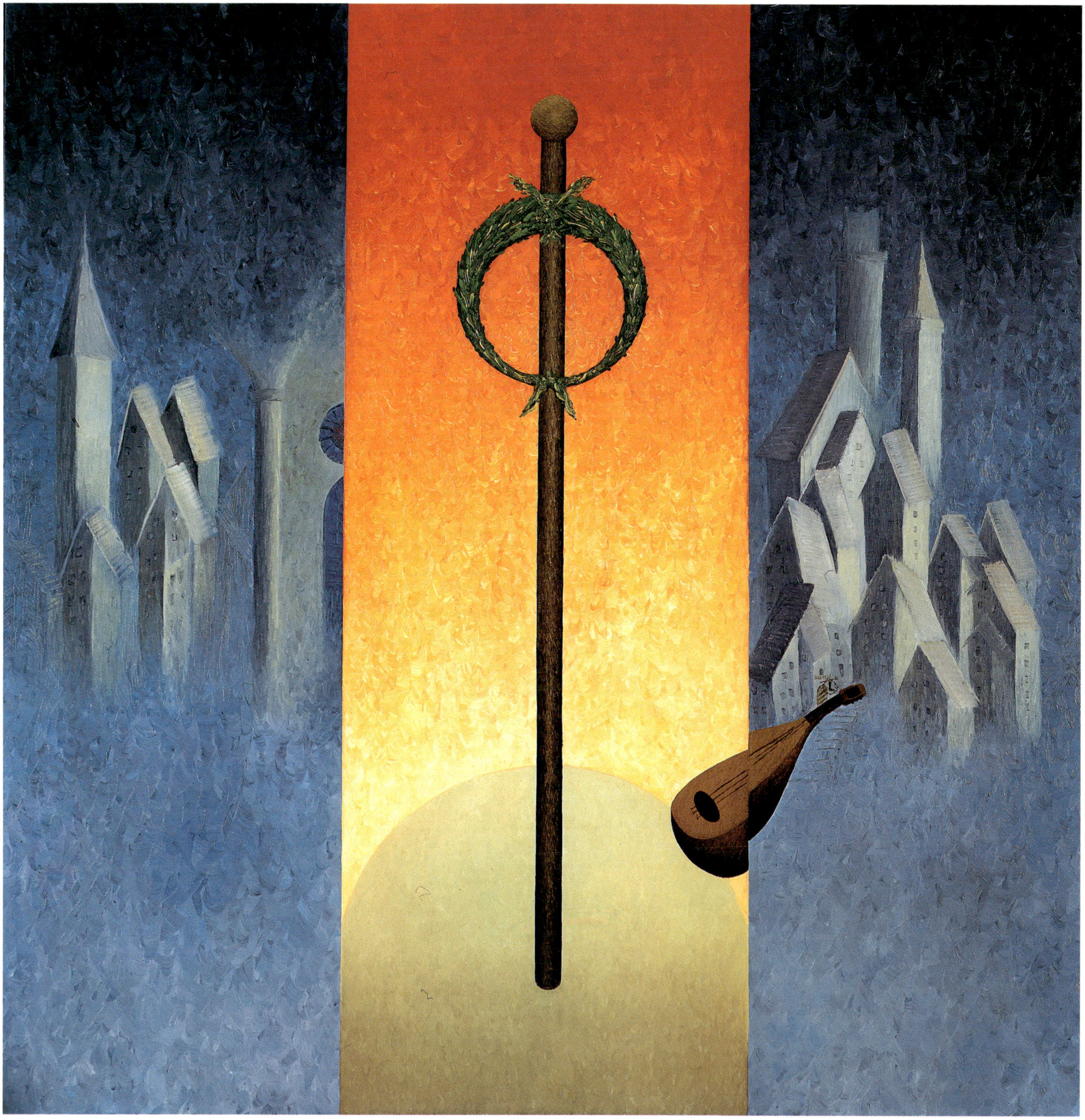

BAUDELAIRE ONCE REMARKED "faire l'amour c'est faire le mal." Sex had always been associated with vice in Wagner's mind. Because of their sense of guilt, Baudelaire and his followers were attracted to Wagner's satanic tale of Tannhäuser. They soon made Wagner a part of the French Decadent and Symbolist movements of the 19th century. It was Wagner's intimate knowledge of the opera, gained during his production of Tannhäuser, that provided the impetus for the idea of the festival house at Bayreuth.

Wagner had great respect for the soul of the antique world and he revered Greek philology. He did not write anything in this field that did not reflect the Apollonian and Dionysiac principles as the two central organizing elements of Greek culture. It is ironic that Nietzsche completed the first part of Zarathustra during the same hours that Wagner died in Venice. When Nietzsche received the news of Wagner's death he wrote to Frantz Overbeck "Wagner was on the whole the most human man that I knew, but there was something between us that could get worse if he lived longer."

TANNHAUSER.

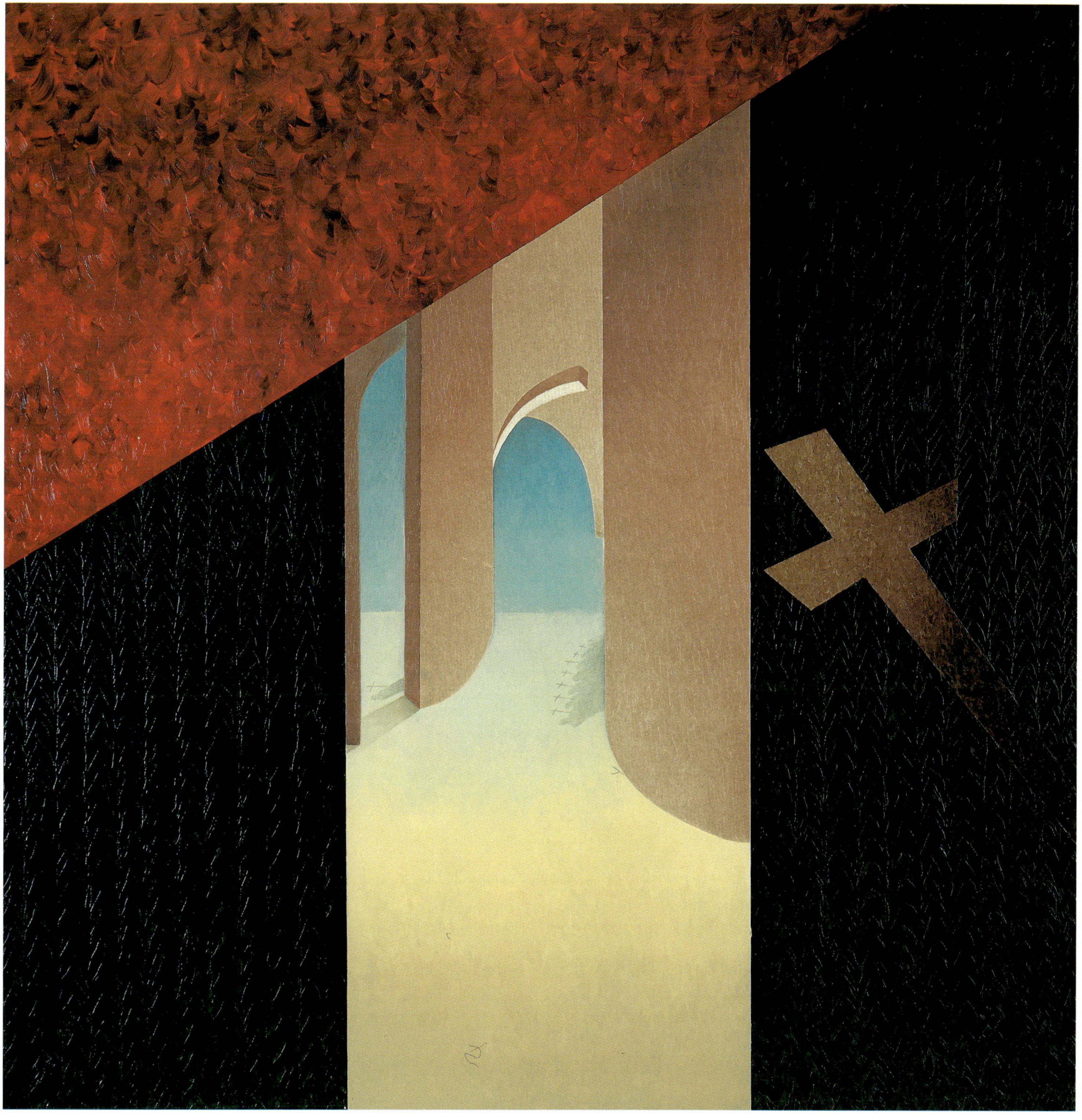

IT WAS ON CHRISTMAS EVE, 1869, in Triebschen that Wagner shared his formative ideas about Parsifal with Nietzsche. Nietzsche was surprised that Wagner had found “another Walter von Stoltzing” and wrote to Peter Gast, “you understand me very well . . . I have not any love or admiration for Parsifal.” Nietzsche later wrote, “Scarcely anyone has character sufficient to resist being undone – being ’redeemed’ – when he perceives himself treated as a god; thereupon he condescends to women. A man is cowardly before the Eternal Feminine, and women (die Wiebling) know it.”

Nietzsche was obviously referring to the relationship between Richard and Cosima. Wagner had adopted the fierce misogyny of Schopenhauer, the great ”Frauenhasser.” According to this view, women are seen as demonic, destructive, and evil; and the aged Wagner sought to free himself from its grasp. He found this hard, suffocating, even Strindbergian. Cosima so often behaved absurdly, reminding us of Wilhelm Busch’s “Promme Helene.” The heights of deviltry and the depths of atonement between which Kundry travels perhaps echoed her creator’s frequent and passionate outbursts against his wife.

Wagner was very sensitive to the sacred nature of Parsifal and when one of the members of the chorus laughed during a rehearsal, Wagner exclaimed, “You leave the stage immediately! A man who can laugh now is not a good human being and has therefore nothing to do here!”

PARSIFAL.

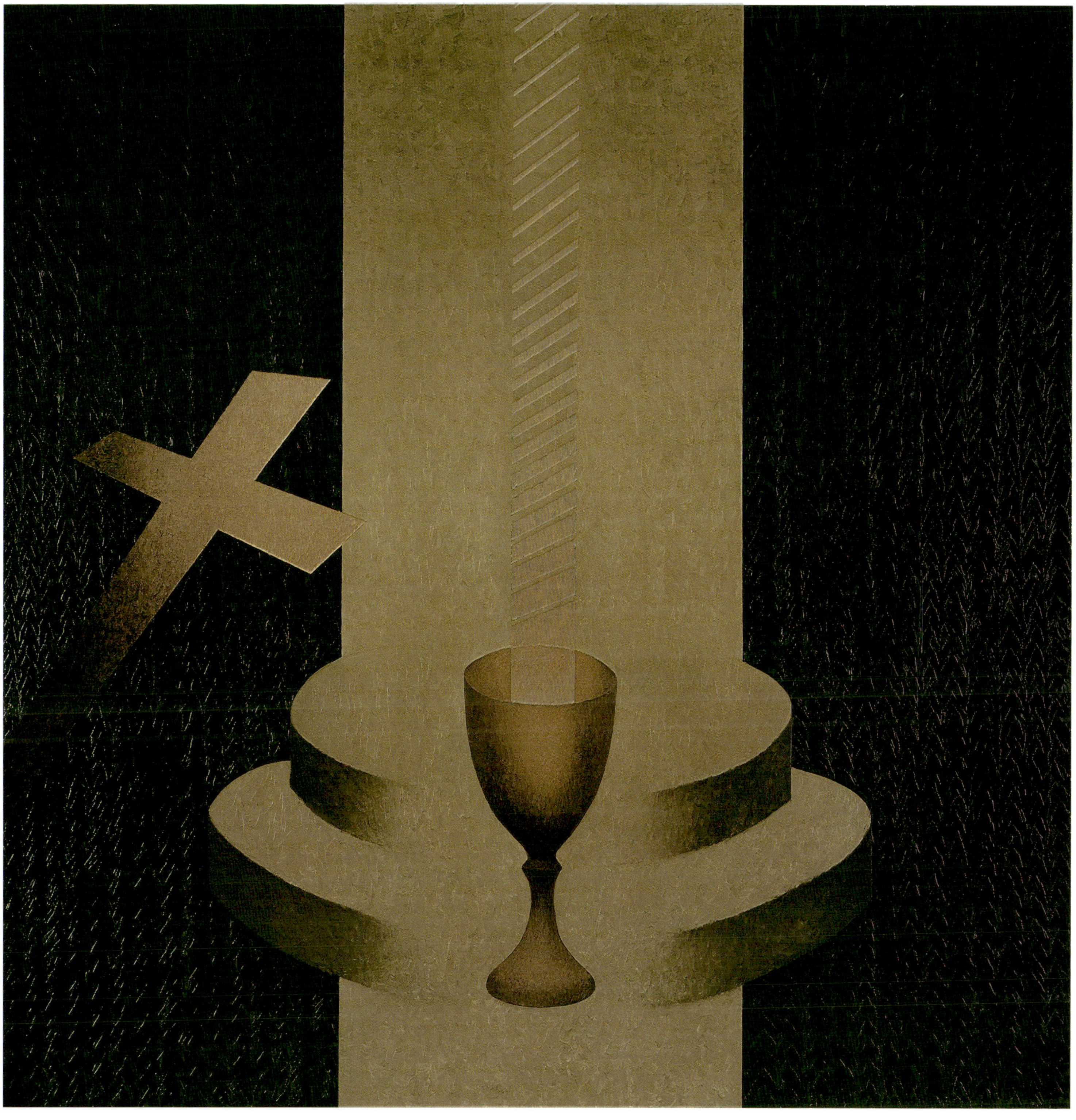

Biographical notes

James A. Mason

James A. Mason retired from Brigham Young University in 1997 after serving as the founding director of the Museum of Art. During his forty years at the university, eleven were spent as dean of the College of Fine Arts and Communications. He is professor emeritus of music and former chairman of that department.

He has been a visiting professor at Indiana University, University of Texas, and Northwestern University. He has lectured in Beijing, China, and Warsaw, Poland, and was a consultant in Kiev, Ukraine on western concepts in higher education programs.

Dr. Mason has chaired national symposia and worked with a number of national committees in developing more effective arts programs, including two White House Conferences and the Ford Foundation's Comprehensive Music Program.

Throughout his varied career, he has received a number of awards.

Dr. Mason was elected national president of the 65,000-member Music Educational National Conference? and served in Washington for his two-year term. He was co-founder of The Board of Trustees for the Utah Opera and the Utah Symphony Orchestra.

Providing Brigham Young University with an art museum is the crowning achievement of Dr. Mason's career at the university. He was the driving force for building the Museum of Art and for raising the donated funds that made his dream of a great art museum on the BYU Campus a reality.

James A. Mason drog sig nyligen tillbaka i pension från Brigham Young University där han var direktör och grundare av Museum of Art. Under elva av fyrtio år vid universitetet var han Dean (dekanus) vid College of Fine Arts and Communications. Han är professor emeritus i musik och tidigare ordförande för denna institution.

Han har varit gästprofessor vid Indiana University, University of Texas and Nothwestern University. Han har föreläst i Peking och Warzawa och varit konsult i Kiev inom området västerländska koncept för högre utbldningsprogram.

Dr. Mason har varit ordförande för internationella symposier och har arbetat i ett antal kommittéer med syfte att utveckla effektivare konstprogram. Här kan särskilt nämnas två White House Conferences samt Ford Foundation's Comprehensive Music Program.

Dr. Mason valdes till president för Music Educational National Conference med 65 000 medlemmar och tjänstgjorde här under två år i Washington. Han var en av grundarna till The Board of Trustees for the Utah Opera.

För Dr Mason utgör skapandet av ett konstmuseum för Brigham Young University höjdpunkten på hans verksamhet vid universitetet. Han var den pådrivande kraften vid både finansieringen och byggandet, samtidigt som hans dröm om ett magnifikt konstmuseum uppfylldes.

Erland Josephson

Born on June 15, 1923, in Stockholm. Character lead of the Swedish stage and screen, notable for his portraits of egocentric males in the films of Ingmar Bergman. He became associated with Bergman while still in his teens and became his lifelong friend. He created parts in Bergman films like *Scenes from a marriage, Cries and Whispers, Fanny and Alexander.* Writing under the nom de plume of Buntel Erik, Josephson co-scripted Bergman's *The Pleasure Garden and All These Women*, and under his own name has written nine novels, poems, and plays. He has also published five autobiographical works. Recently he published *Mr Silberstein* in English.

In 1966 he was appointed head of Stockholm's Royal Dramatic Theater, a position he held through 1975.

Extremely active in films outside his native Sweden, Josephson's most famous non-Bergman film role was in the U.S. production *The Unbearable Lightness of Being.* He worked with directors such as Andrej Tarkovskij, Lilliana Cavani, Istvan Szabo, Theo Angelopoulos and Peter Brook.

He made his American stage debut in a 1988 production of *The Cherry Orchard.*

(In 1977 he was awarded an honorary doctorate from the University of Stockholm.)

Erland Josephson föddes den 15 juni 1923 i Stockholm. Han är en ledande svensk karaktärskådespelare inom teater och film. Han har särskilt uppmärksammats för sina rollporträtt av starkt egocentriska män i Ingmar Bergmans filmer. En vänskapskontakt med Ingmar Bergman knöts redan i ungdomen och har utvecklats till en livslång arbetsgemenskap. Josephson har gjort stora roller i många av Bergmans filmer som t ex Scener ur ett äktenskap, Viskningar och rop *och* Fanny och Alexander.

Under pseudonymen Buntel Erik medarbetade han som manusförfattare i andra av Bergmans filmer som Lustgården *eller* För att inte tala om alla dessa kvinnor.

Under eget namn har Josephson publicerat nio romaner, ett antal skådespel och poesi. Han har också givit ut fem självbiografiska verk och nyligen har den första översättningen till engelska lanserats – Mr Silberstein.

1966 efterträdde han Bergman som chef för Kungliga Dramatiska Teatern i Stockholm. Ett post som Josephson upprätthöll till 1975.

Josephson har bedrivit en betydande internationell verksamhet. Den mest framträdande rollen i en "icke-bergman-film" var Varats olidliga lätthet. *Han har arbetat tillsammans med regissörer som Andrej Tarkovskij, Lilliana Cavani, Istvan Szabo, Theo Angelopoulos and Peter Brook.*

Han gjorde sin amerikanska scendebut 1988 i en uppsättning av Körsbärsträdgården.

(1977 utnämndes han till hedersdoktor vid Stockholms Universitet.)

Karl Momen

Swedish artist Karl Momen was born in 1934 near the Russian border in Mashhad, Iran. He began to paint when he was seven years old. Painter Urie Popow offered Karl art lessons. Popow had been an influential avant-garde painter in Russia before the Revolution. He introduced Karl to the work of Kazimir Malevich (1878-1935), Vladimir Tatlin (1885-1953), El Lissitzky, (1890-1941), as well as other Russian Constructivists, and Suprematists. Karl did not know who these painters were at the time and could not understand why they would paint abstract geometric images, but he was intrigued by their work.

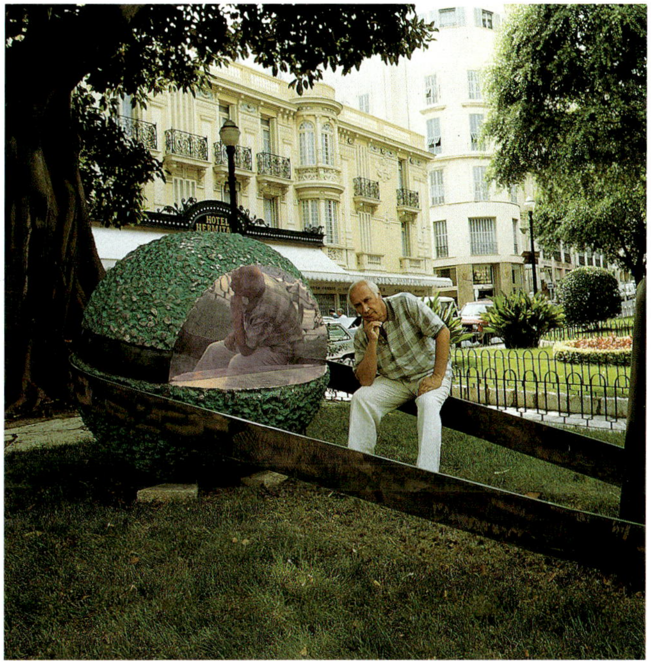

Catapult *at the 2nd biennal de Monaco, 1989. Photo by Marcel Loli.*

At the age of fifteen, Karl was commissioned to paint a six-foot high official portrait of Stalin. Some years later, when the Shah of Iran returned to power, Momen was commissioned to paint a similar portrait of the Shah twelve feet high. Following the completion of his academic education in 1954, and military service at the academy in Tehran, he traveled to Stuttgart, Germany, to begin his studies in architecture at the Kunst Academy. A few years later he met Max Ernst (1891-1975), a guest professor at the Academy, and they established a long-standing friendship.

Momen completed his training in art and architecture, first in Germany and then in Sweden. A highly respected architect in Stockholm, he gave up his architectural work and devoted himself entirely to art. He occupied himself supplying a waiting list of over forty European companies with paintings and sculptures produced under his hand.

He held important solo exhibitions in New York, Tokyo, Berlin, Stockholm, Monte Carlo, and Salt Lake City. Exhibitions of his paintings and sculpture may be found at various museums, art centers, culture centers in Europe, Japan, and the United States. Momen has acquired a residence studio in the area of San Francisco, California, to escape the harsh Swedish winters.

First edition sponsored by:

LIVIA

LIVIA is a true virtual life insurance company competing in a nonvirtual environment. Simplicity and cost efficiency are key words. LIVIA is a subsidiary to Merita Nordbanken, a major bank in the Nordic area.
http://www.livia.se

AmericanAirlines®

American Airlines is one of the largest airlines in the world with a total revenue of $17,8 billion in 1996.
American Airlines has a daily non-stop service from Stockholm to Chicago with connectins to more than 200 cities in the US and South America.

OM VPA AB

OM VPA, a securities company within the OM Group, specializes in settlement services and related software development. The OM Group runs securities and derivatives exchanges in Stockholm and London and acts as an international supplier of related transaction technology.